הגדה של פסח

ENGLISH COMMENTARIES
EDITED BY

Marion Wiesel

Simon & Schuster Paperbacks

NEW YORK   LONDON   TORONTO   SYDNEY

A Passover Haggadah

AS COMMENTED UPON BY

Elie Wiesel

AND ILLUSTRATED BY

Mark Podwal

SIMON & SCHUSTER PAPERBACKS
Rockefeller Center
1230 Avenue of the Americas
New York, NY 10020

This Simon & Schuster paperback edition 2006

SIMON & SCHUSTER PAPERBACKS and colophon are
registered trademarks of Simon & Schuster, Inc.

For information regarding special discounts for bulk purchases,
please contact Simon & Schuster Special Sales :
1-800-456-6798 or business@simonandschuster.com

Designed by Levavi & Levavi, Inc.
Hebrew typesetting by EL OT Ltd., Tel Aviv
English typesetting by Dix Type, Syracuse
Manufactured in the United States of America

30 29 28 27 26 25 24

Library of Congress Cataloging-in-Publication Data
Haggadah. English & Hebrew.
  A Passover Haggadah / as commented upon by Elie Wiesel and
illustrated by Mark Podwal.
    p.   cm.
  1. Haggadot—Texts.   2. Seder—Liturgy—Texts.   3. Judaism—
Liturgy—Texts. 4. Haggadah. I. Wiesel, Elie, 1928–
II. Podwal, Mark H., 1945– III. Title.
BM674.643.W54   1993
296.4'37—dc20   92-31988

ISBN-13 978-0-671-73541-8
ISBN-10:   0-671-73541-1
ISBN-13: 978-0-671-79996-0 (Pbk.)
ISBN-10:   0-671-79996-7 (Pbk.)

Preface

Like most Jewish children, I especially loved the Passover holiday. Solemn and joyous, it allowed us to escape time. Slaves of the pharaohs, we followed Moses into the unknown, into the desert, up to Mount Sinai. His summons to freedom was stronger than fear.

The Seder transformed us. On that evening, my father enjoyed the sovereignty of a king. My mother, lovelier than ever, was queen. And we, the children, were princes. Even visitors—the travelers and beggars we had invited to share our meal—were messengers bearing secrets, princes in disguise.

How could I not love this holiday, which began well before the Seder itself. For weeks, we lived in a state of expectancy, of preparation.

The house had to be cleaned, the books removed to the courtyard for dusting. The rabbi's disciples assisted in making the matzot. Passover meant the end of winter, the triumph of spring.

Here I must interrupt my tale, for I see that I am using the past tense. Why? Because none of this is true anymore? Not at all. The meaning of the festival and its rituals has scarcely changed. Only I have changed.

I still follow the rituals, of course. I recite the prayers, I chant the appropriate psalms, I tell the story of the Exodus, I answer the questions my son asks. But in the deepest part of myself, I know it is not the same. It is not as it used to be.

A lifetime separates me from the child I once was. Today I know that happiness can never be complete. The joyousness of this holiday is so tinged with melancholy that it seems more like a time of sadness.

It is understandable; Passover was the last holiday I celebrated at home.

I recall this to explain why it is impossible for me to talk about Passover solely in the present tense.

Do I love it less than before? No. Let's just say I love it differently. Now I love it for the questions it raises, which are, after all, its *raison d'être.*

What is most appealing about the Seder? Its challenge to children to ask questions. "Why is this night different from all other nights?" Because it reminds us of another night, so long ago, yet so near, the last night a persecuted and oppressed people, our people, spent in Egypt. "Why do we eat bitter herbs?" To remind us of the bitter tears that our forefathers shed in exile. Each song, each gesture, each cup of wine, each prayer, each silence is part of the evening's spell. The goal is to arouse our curiosity by opening the doors of memory.

On this evening, all questions are not only permitted, but invited. Still, we begin by examining the traditional four questions which illustrate four possible attitudes toward life: that of the wise son, who knows the question and asks it; that of the wicked son, who knows the question but refuses to ask it; that of the simple son, who knows the question but is indifferent to it; and finally, that of the ignorant son, who does not know the question and therefore is unable to ask.

And then, there is my own anguish: What can we do so as not to forget the question? What can we do to defeat oblivion? What significance does Passover have, if not to keep our memories alive? To be Jewish is to assume the burden of the past, to include it in our concerns for the present and for the future.

We read the news and it is always the same: random killings in Jerusalem, confrontations in Hebron, bombings in Lebanon.

Were it not for its past and its history—or rather our connection to its history—what right would we have to Jerusalem, or to the land of Israel itself? If events in the Mideast have any meaning, it is as a reminder of the need to remember. The peace between Israel and Egypt strikes us as miraculous not only because of Sadat and Begin, but because of Moses.

As we recite the Haggadah, which retells the Exodus of the Children of Israel from Egypt, we have the strange feeling that, once again, we are living in Biblical times.

More than any generation before, my contemporaries have known not only a paroxysm of evil, but *also* the realization of a promise; not only the Kingdom of Night, but *also* the rebirth of a dream; not only the horror of Nazism, but *also* the end of the nightmare; not only the deaths of Babi-Yar, but *also* the defiance of young Russian Jews, the first to challenge the Kremlin's police state.

Sometimes the sheer speed of events makes us reel. History advances at a dizzying pace. Man has conquered space, but not his own heart. Have we learned nothing? It seems so: Witness the wars that rage all over the globe, the acts of terror that strike down the innocent, the children who are dying of hunger and disease in Africa and Asia every day. Why is there so much hatred in the world? Why is there so much indifference to hatred, to suffering, to the anguish of others?

I love Passover because for me it is a cry against indifference, a cry for compassion.

Listen to a story about Job, who lived in Egypt in the time of Moses. He held the important position of adviser in the Pharaoh's court, along with Jethro and Bilaam. When the Pharaoh asked for counsel in resolving the Jewish question, Jethro spoke in favor of Moses' request to let his people go. Bilaam took the opposite stand. As for Job, he refused to take sides; he wished to remain neutral. This neutrality, the Midrash says, earned him his future sufferings. At times of crisis, at moments of peril, one has no right

to choose abstention, to opt for prudence. When the life or death —or simply the well-being—of a community is at stake, neutrality becomes unacceptable, for it always aids and abets the oppressor, never his victim.

The second story is no less provocative. It can be found in the Midrash, in the passage about the Red Sea crossing. The Children of Israel are saved at the last moment, while their oppressors drown before their eyes. It is a moment of grace so extraordinary that the angels themselves begin to sing, but God interrupts and scolds them: What has come over you? My creatures are drowning in the sea and you are singing? How can you praise me with your hymns at a time when human beings are dying?

Although neither of these stories is part of the traditional Seder, I like to tell them.

Oh, I know—it is easier said than done. Compassion for the enemies of one's people—who has the right to advance such a proposition? It may be an option for God and angels, but for humans? Then why this story? To prompt us to question. If God demands compassion, then it is our responsibility to take a stand, even if it is to say, no, not yet . . . but later, perhaps.

Still, I have seen Israel at war, and I can attest to the fact that there was no hatred for enemy soldiers. Yes, there was a fierce determination to win, but no hatred.

At the time, I remember how difficult it was for me to understand this phenomenon; it seemed illogical, irrational. When an enemy seeks to destroy you, you need to feel as much hatred for him as he feels for you. All of military history proves it. But all of Jewish history proves the contrary. The Jewish people have never had recourse to hatred, even in their struggles for survival.

Surely that was a blessing. If we had had to hate all our enemies, we would have had little time or energy for anything else.

And so I return to the last holiday I celebrated at home with my family in my small town tucked away in the Carpathian Mountains. By then, the region was infested with Germans. In Buda-

pest, they were already planning the deportation and liquidation of our communities, only we did not know it. The Russian front seemed close; at night, we heard the cannons, we saw the sky turn red and we thought that soon we would be free.

The authorities had forbidden communal prayer in the synagogues, so we arranged to hold services in our house. Normally, on Passover eve, we would chant the melodies with great fervor. Not this time. This time we only murmured the words.

I remember that Seder, and I shall always remember it. Heads bowed, we silently evoked old memories. We hardly dared ask ourselves if God would intervene to save us.

He had not often intervened in the past. Would He this time?

Passover is also a story of hope.

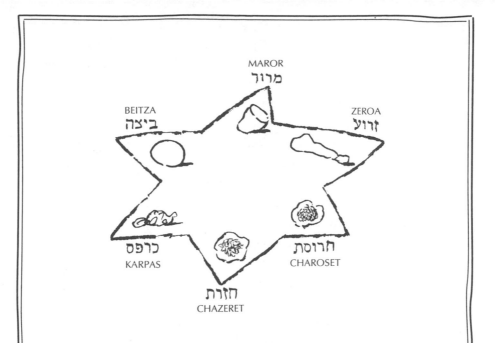

The entire story of the Haggadah is contained in the Seder plate; everything on it symbolizes an aspect of Exodus:

(1) ZEROA, a roasted bone, evokes the Paschal lamb which our forefathers offered to God.

(2) BEITZA, a boiled egg whose roundness symbolizes the circle of life and death.

(3) MAROR, a bitter herb, reminds us of the bitterness of Egyptian bondage.

(4) CHAROSET, a mixture of nuts, fruit, wine, and spices, represents the mortar our ancestors used in building the pyramids in Egypt.

(5) KARPAS, parsley or another green vegetable, represents hope and renewal.

(6) CHAZERET, the bitter herb for the "sandwich" which we eat later, following the custom established by Hillel the Elder, as a reminder that our ancestors "ate matzah and bitter herbs together."

The Seder

KADESH	Reciting the Kiddush	קַדֵּשׁ
U'RECHATZ	Washing of the hands	וּרְחַץ
KARPAS	Blessing for the green vegetable	כַּרְפַּס
YACHATZ	Breaking of the middle matzah	יַחַץ
MAGGID	Telling the story	מַגִּיד
RACHTZAH	Washing the hands before the meal	רָחְצָה
MOTZI MATZAH	Prayer for the beginning of the meal and blessing for the matzah	מוֹצִיא מַצָּה
MAROR	Blessing for the bitter herbs	מָרוֹר
KORECH	Hillel's sandwich	כּוֹרֵךְ
SHULCHAN ORECH	The meal	שֻׁלְחָן עוֹרֵךְ
TZAFUN	The afikoman	צָפוּן
BARECH	Saying grace	בָּרֵךְ
HALLEL	Psalms of praise	הַלֵּל
NIRTZAH	Conclusion of the service	נִרְצָה

11

The Seder

"This is the bread of affliction which our forefathers ate in the land of Egypt. Let all those who are hungry come and eat with us. . . ."

Thus begins the Seder, that ancient family ceremony in which Jews the world over join in reliving an event that took place thirty-five centuries ago.

To ensure that the opening invitation of the Haggadah was understood by all, the text began not in Hebrew, but in Aramaic, the everyday language of our ancestors. Later, our medieval sages urged that the Seder be conducted in the language of the participants, since comprehension of the text is vital. The great book of Kabbalah, the Zohar, provides an additional reason for the Haggadah to begin in Aramaic: It tells us that God Himself likes to hear His children recount the story of the Exodus from Egypt. And so we begin in Aramaic, which the angels do not understand, speaking directly to God without intermediaries.

The Seder is, above all, a story. Our story. It belongs to all of us. In New York and Paris, Casablanca and Jerusalem, wherever Jews are Jews, we perform the same rituals tonight. We invoke the same images, eat the same matzot, and together welcome our illustrious visitor, the prophet Elijah.

Through the centuries, the Seder has come to embrace styles and practices of various traditions. Certain Oriental communities open the evening with a dramatic rendering of the story: A man enters dressed as a wanderer, carrying a bag on his shoulders. Someone at the table—a child, perhaps—asks him where he

12

comes from. "From the land of Egypt," he replies. "Where are you going?" "To the land of my ancestors," he says. They all exclaim, "Next year in Jerusalem." He is invited to sit down, and only then do they begin the narrative.

Let us start together.

קַדֵּשׁ

Kadesh

RECITING THE KIDDUSH

In the Jewish tradition, every ceremony begins with the Kiddush. The wine is sanctified with this ancient ritual to mark the beginning of the festive meal. Jews are reminded of their need for saintliness, and they, in turn, remind the Almighty of His professed eternal love for His people.

Gathered around the candlelit table, we bless God for having released us from Egyptian slavery and sanctified us with His commandments, for offering us occasions to celebrate our holidays, and for allowing us to evoke our glorious past, when three times a year—during Passover, Shavuot, and Sukkot—the inhabitants of Judea made pilgrimages to the holy convocations in the holiest of all cities, Jerusalem.

The Kiddush is said over the first of the four cups of wine that one drinks during the Seder. The number is symbolic. Scripture uses four words to describe the liberation from Egypt; they refer to the four exiles the Jewish people will endure in its history, all four ending in redemption. Thus, to drink the four cups of wine is a commandment as important as to eat matzah or bitter herbs.

If the Seder takes place on the Sabbath eve, the Kiddush begins with the text of Genesis describing the end of the sixth day and the arrival of the seventh. We are required to stand as we recite or listen to this Biblical passage. Why? Because in listening to

God's word we testify to its truth. And because, according to the Bible, a witness must testify standing.

The first cup of wine is poured. The head of the table, holding the cup in his right hand, recites the following, beginning with the bracketed Biblical passage if the Seder falls on Friday night. It is followed by related commentary, also in brackets.

(וַיְהִי עֶרֶב וַיְהִי בֹקֶר

יוֹם הַשִּׁשִּׁי. וַיְכֻלּוּ הַשָּׁמַיִם וְהָאָרֶץ וְכָל צְבָאָם. וַיְכַל אֱלֹהִים בַּיּוֹם הַשְּׁבִיעִי מְלַאכְתּוֹ אֲשֶׁר עָשָׂה, וַיִּשְׁבֹּת בַּיּוֹם הַשְּׁבִיעִי מִכָּל מְלַאכְתּוֹ אֲשֶׁר עָשָׂה. וַיְבָרֶךְ אֱלֹהִים אֶת יוֹם הַשְּׁבִיעִי וַיְקַדֵּשׁ אֹתוֹ, כִּי בוֹ שָׁבַת מִכָּל מְלַאכְתּוֹ, אֲשֶׁר בָּרָא אֱלֹהִים לַעֲשׂוֹת.)

[Evening came and morning came, the sixth day. The heavens, the earth, and all they contain were completed. On the seventh day, God rested from all the work He had done and everything He had made. And God blessed the seventh day and made it holy, because it was the day on which He rested from all His work of Creation.]

[Thus, all of Creation joined in that rest, as rest, too, became part of Creation. And time was consecrated. The Sabbath is God's gift to humanity, a sanctuary in time. Israel's very survival is linked to it. Israel will maintain the Sabbath and in the end, the Sabbath will maintain Israel.]

סָבְרִי מָרָנָן וְרַבּוֹתַי.

בָּרוּךְ אַתָּה יְיָ אֱלֹהֵינוּ מֶלֶךְ הָעוֹלָם בּוֹרֵא
פְּרִי הַגָּפֶן.

Blessed are You, Lord our God, King of the Universe, who creates the fruit of the vine.

בָּרוּךְ אַתָּה יְיָ אֱלֹהֵינוּ מֶלֶךְ הָעוֹלָם אֲשֶׁר בָּחַר בָּנוּ מִכָּל עָם

וְרוֹמְמָנוּ מִכָּל לָשׁוֹן וְקִדְּשָׁנוּ בְּמִצְוֹתָיו. וַתִּתֶּן לָנוּ, יְיָ אֱלֹהֵינוּ,

בְּאַהֲבָה (שַׁבָּתוֹת לִמְנוּחָה וּ)מוֹעֲדִים לְשִׂמְחָה, חַגִּים וּזְמַנִּים

לְשָׂשׂוֹן, אֶת יוֹם (הַשַּׁבָּת הַזֶּה, וְאֶת יוֹם) חַג הַמַּצּוֹת הַזֶּה, זְמַן

חֵרוּתֵנוּ, (בְּאַהֲבָה) מִקְרָא קֹדֶשׁ, זֵכֶר לִיצִיאַת מִצְרָיִם. כִּי בָנוּ

בָחַרְתָּ, וְאוֹתָנוּ קִדַּשְׁתָּ מִכָּל הָעַמִּים (וְשַׁבָּת) וּמוֹעֲדֵי קָדְשֶׁךָ

(בְּאַהֲבָה וּבְרָצוֹן) בְּשִׂמְחָה וּבְשָׂשׂוֹן הִנְחַלְתָּנוּ. בָּרוּךְ אַתָּה יְיָ

מְקַדֵּשׁ (הַשַּׁבָּת וְ)יִשְׂרָאֵל וְהַזְּמַנִּים.

Blessed are You, Lord our God, King of the Universe, who has chosen us among peoples, exalted us among nations, and sanctified us with His laws. You have lovingly given us [Sabbaths for rest] holy days and festivals for joy and rejoicing. This [Sabbath day and this] day of the festival of matzah, the time of our libera-

tion [with love], a holy convocation in memory of our leaving Egypt. For You have chosen us and sanctified us among all peoples by giving us [the Sabbath and] holy days [in love and favor] as a joyous inheritance. Blessed are You, Lord, who sanctifies [the Sabbath and] Israel and the seasons.

On Saturday night the following prayer is added to acknowledge the conclusion of the Sabbath:

(בָּרוּךְ אַתָּה יְיָ אֱלֹהֵינוּ מֶלֶךְ הָעוֹלָם בּוֹרֵא מְאוֹרֵי הָאֵשׁ.

[Blessed are You, Lord our God, King of the Universe, who creates the light of fire.

בָּרוּךְ אַתָּה יְיָ אֱלֹהֵינוּ מֶלֶךְ הָעוֹלָם הַמַּבְדִּיל בֵּין קֹדֶשׁ לְחֹל, בֵּין אוֹר לְחֹשֶׁךְ, בֵּין יִשְׂרָאֵל לָעַמִּים, בֵּין יוֹם הַשְּׁבִיעִי לְשֵׁשֶׁת יְמֵי הַמַּעֲשֶׂה. בֵּין קְדֻשַּׁת שַׁבָּת לִקְדֻשַּׁת יוֹם טוֹב הִבְדַּלְתָּ, וְאֶת יוֹם הַשְּׁבִיעִי מִשֵּׁשֶׁת יְמֵי הַמַּעֲשֶׂה קִדַּשְׁתָּ; הִבְדַּלְתָּ וְקִדַּשְׁתָּ אֶת עַמְּךָ יִשְׂרָאֵל בִּקְדֻשָּׁתֶךָ. בָּרוּךְ אַתָּה יְיָ הַמַּבְדִּיל בֵּין קֹדֶשׁ לְקֹדֶשׁ.)

Blessed are You, Lord our God, King of the Universe, who distinguishes between the sacred and the mundane, between light and

darkness, between Israel and other nations, between the seventh day of rest and the six days of toil. You have distinguished between the sanctity of the Sabbath and the sanctity of a festival, and You have sanctified the seventh day above the six days of work. You have distinguished and sanctified Israel with Your own holiness. Blessed are You, Lord, our God, who distinguishes between Holy and Holy.]

As always on festive occasions, one is duty bound to recite the following prayer:

בָּרוּךְ אַתָּה יְיָ אֱלֹהֵינוּ מֶלֶךְ הָעוֹלָם שֶׁהֶחֱיָנוּ
וְקִיְּמָנוּ וְהִגִּיעָנוּ לַזְּמַן הַזֶּה.

Blessed are You, Lord our God, King of the Universe, who has kept us alive and sustained us and allowed us to reach this season.

All drink the first cup of wine while reclining.

וּרְחַץ

U'rechatz

WASHING OF THE HANDS

A pitcher, a basin, and a towel are readied so that the head of the table may wash his hands.

[He is served first because tonight he is king in his home. Leaning back on a cushion like a citizen of ancient Rome, he enjoys the privileges of sovereignty. He is a free man who remembers. And who is free because he remembers.]

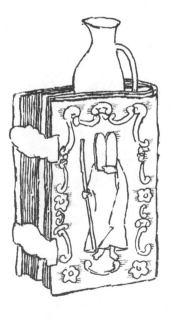

כַּרְפַּס

Karpas

BLESSING FOR THE GREEN VEGETABLE

We dip parsley, celery, or lettuce in saltwater and recite the prayer:

בָּרוּךְ אַתָּה יְיָ אֱלֹהֵינוּ מֶלֶךְ הָעוֹלָם בּוֹרֵא פְּרִי הָאֲדָמָה.

Blessed are You, Lord our God, King of the Universe, who creates the fruit of the earth.

Why do we eat karpas? To encourage the children at the table, and the child within each of us, to ask questions. But why parsley? And why saltwater? This ritual has only one purpose: to excite our curiosity.

יַחַץ

Yachatz

BREAKING OF THE MIDDLE MATZAH

The head of the table takes the middle matzah and breaks it in two. The larger piece, the afikoman, is wrapped in a napkin and hidden from the children. It is needed for the end of the meal, when the children will exchange it for a gift. The smaller piece is replaced between the two other matzot.

The larger piece of the matzah represents *lachma anya,* the bread of the poor. It is meant to remind us of the hungry.

At that moment, we should identify with those who are afraid to eat their bread, and always leave something for later. After all, weren't we all wretched as slaves in Egypt?

מַגִּיד

Maggid

TELLING THE STORY

The matzot are uncovered and raised for all to see as we recite:

הָא לַחְמָא עַנְיָא דִּי אֲכַלוּ אַבְהָתָנָא בְּאַרְעָא דְמִצְרָיִם. כָּל דִּכְפִין יֵיתֵי וְיֵיכֹל, כָּל דִּצְרִיךְ יֵיתֵי וְיִפְסַח. הָשַׁתָּא הָכָא, לְשָׁנָה הַבָּאָה בְּאַרְעָא דְיִשְׂרָאֵל. הָשַׁתָּא עַבְדֵי, לְשָׁנָה הַבָּאָה בְּנֵי חוֹרִין.

This is the bread of affliction
which our forefathers ate in the land of Egypt.
Let all those who are hungry come and eat with us.
Let all those who are in need come and share our meal.
This year we are here.
Next year may we all be in the land of Israel.
This year we are still slaves.
Next year may we all be free.

The matzot are covered.

A memory from my town, Sighet: Our Seder table was never without a stranger. I remember that we went from one synagogue to the other, from one house of study to the other, looking for a stranger without whom our holiday would be incomplete. And this was true of most Jews in my town and probably of most Jews in other towns. On Passover eve, the poor, the uprooted, the unhappy were the most sought-after, the most beloved guests. It was for them and with them that we recited: "This year we are still slaves. Next year may we all be free." Without comforting our impoverished guest, our riches would shame us. And so we were grateful to him. In some towns, before Passover, Jews would raise funds discreetly: One by one, they would enter a room in the community house. There they would find a dish filled with money. Those who had money left some; those who needed money took some. No one knew how much was given or how much was taken. Thus, the needy were taken care of with dignity.

מַה נִּשְׁתַּנָּה הַלַּיְלָה הַזֶּה מִכָּל הַלֵּילוֹת. שֶׁבְּכָל הַלֵּילוֹת אָנוּ אוֹכְלִין חָמֵץ וּמַצָּה, הַלַּיְלָה הַזֶּה כֻּלּוֹ מַצָּה. שֶׁבְּכָל הַלֵּילוֹת אָנוּ אוֹכְלִין שְׁאָר יְרָקוֹת, הַלַּיְלָה הַזֶּה מָרוֹר. שֶׁבְּכָל הַלֵּילוֹת אֵין אָנוּ מַטְבִּילִין אֲפִלּוּ פַּעַם אֶחָת, הַלַּיְלָה הַזֶּה שְׁתֵּי פְעָמִים. שֶׁבְּכָל הַלֵּילוֹת אָנוּ אוֹכְלִין בֵּין יוֹשְׁבִין וּבֵין מְסֻבִּין, הַלַּיְלָה הַזֶּה כֻּלָּנוּ מְסֻבִּין.

How does this night differ from all other nights? On all other nights we eat either leavened or unleavened bread. Why on this night do we eat only unleavened bread?

On all other nights we eat all kinds of herbs. Why on this night do we eat only bitter herbs?

On all other nights we need not dip our herbs even once. Why on this night do we need to dip twice?

On all other nights we eat either sitting or reclining. Why on this night must we all recline?

These questions are simple and practical. As said before, the entire Seder has been conceived for children. We must teach them how to ask questions. And therefore, for guidance, we offer them the proverbial Four Questions. Then, it is up to each child to ask his own.

Commentators have found all kinds of secret meanings in the Four Questions. According to Don Yitzhak Abrabanel, the great Spanish sage, the questions deal with the contradictions that govern Jewish life in exile. More specifically, there are mystical scholars who assert that leavened bread symbolizes the evil spirit, whereas matzah represents purity of the soul. Perhaps. We are all entitled to our own interpretation. For the learned, the Seder offers the possibility of further study. For the novice, it affords the pleasures of a simple story. Children will begin by wanting to understand the nature of what they see and hear, what they touch and taste. Later their questions will become more complex: Why exile? Why suffering? Why evil? And who can explain why they prevail? Here, then, is the answer offered since the beginning of exile:

עֲבָדִים הָיִינוּ לְפַרְעֹה בְּמִצְרָיִם. וַיּוֹצִיאֵנוּ יְיָ
אֱלֹהֵינוּ מִשָּׁם, בְּיָד חֲזָקָה וּבִזְרוֹעַ
נְטוּיָה. וְאִלּוּ לֹא הוֹצִיא הַקָּדוֹשׁ בָּרוּךְ הוּא אֶת אֲבוֹתֵינוּ
מִמִּצְרַיִם, הֲרֵי אָנוּ וּבָנֵינוּ וּבְנֵי בָנֵינוּ מְשֻׁעְבָּדִים הָיִינוּ לְפַרְעֹה
בְּמִצְרָיִם. וַאֲפִלוּ כֻּלָּנוּ חֲכָמִים, כֻּלָּנוּ נְבוֹנִים, כֻּלָּנוּ זְקֵנִים,
כֻּלָּנוּ יוֹדְעִים אֶת הַתּוֹרָה, מִצְוָה עָלֵינוּ לְסַפֵּר בִּיצִיאַת מִצְרָיִם.
וְכָל הַמַּרְבֶּה לְסַפֵּר בִּיצִיאַת מִצְרַיִם הֲרֵי זֶה מְשֻׁבָּח.

We were all slaves to Pharaoh in Egypt. And the Lord our God delivered us from there with a mighty hand and an outstretched arm. Had the Holy One, blessed be He, not brought our forefathers out of Egypt, then we, our children, and our children's children, would still be slaves to Pharaoh in Egypt. And even if all of us were scholars, all of us full of understanding, all of us masters, all of us learned in the Torah, we would still be commanded to tell the story of how we left Egypt. And the more one tells the story, with ever more detail and fervor, the greater one's merit.

This statement expresses the essence of Jewish faith, of Jewish allegiance to a collective memory. It is as though we had all been in Egypt together, prisoners of the same enemy, suffering the same pain, the same anguish. It is as though we had all been carried by the same hope.

Even converts must affirm their connection with Egypt, with the experience that preceded our liberation. Is it possible for strangers, sons and daughters of strangers, to have lived in exile as we did? Yes, answers our tradition. In becoming Jewish, converts absorb our entire past, effectively making it their own. Thus we share our memory, going all the way back to Egypt. In exchange, like us, converts must proclaim their faith in divine strength and goodness.

"If God had not brought our forefathers out of Egypt, then we, our children, and our children's children would still be slaves to Pharaoh in Egypt." What a strange statement. The Pharaoh has long ceased to exist. How could we still be his slaves? Clearly, this sentence is allegorical. Pharaohs are not necessarily Egyptian. And Egypt, is not the only place where exile is felt. Each generation has its own enemies, its own struggles and—sometimes—its own victories. We evoke Exodus not only to remember our suffering in Egypt, but also to relive the manner in which we overcame our suffering.

מַעֲשֶׂה בְּרַבִּי אֱלִיעֶזֶר וְרַבִּי יְהוֹשֻׁעַ וְרַבִּי אֶלְעָזָר בֶּן עֲזַרְיָה וְרַבִּי עֲקִיבָא וְרַבִּי טַרְפוֹן, שֶׁהָיוּ מְסֻבִּין בִּבְנֵי בְרַק, וְהָיוּ מְסַפְּרִים בִּיצִיאַת מִצְרַיִם כָּל אוֹתוֹ הַלַּיְלָה, עַד שֶׁבָּאוּ תַלְמִידֵיהֶם וְאָמְרוּ לָהֶם: רַבּוֹתֵינוּ, הִגִּיעַ זְמַן קְרִיאַת שְׁמַע שֶׁל שַׁחֲרִית.

A tale: One Passover eve, Rabbi Eliezer, Rabbi Joshua, Rabbi Elazar ben Azariah, Rabbi Akiba, and Rabbi Tarfon reclined together at B'nai Brak. They told and retold the story of the Exodus from Egypt all through the night, until their disciples came running to tell them: "The time has come to read the morning Sh'ma, the time has come to say the morning prayers."

Why do we tell this story? It teaches us an important lesson. These five sages, among the most illustrious of the Talmud, continued their study of Exodus and the story of that Exodus into the morning hours, even though they were thoroughly familiar with it. Obviously, they wanted to savor every nuance of the narrative—whereas we, who are not so erudite, tend to rush through the story.

Another interpretation: These five sages used the opportunity of the Seder to discuss political problems. Under the pretext of celebrating the Passover meal, they hid from the Romans and discussed the imminent uprising of young warriors in the mountains of Judea against the Roman occupant. By interrupting their masters, the students were signalling that the time for discussion was over; that indeed, the time had come to shout "Sh'ma Israel" publicly and forcefully.

A third interpretation: The students have come not to urge the sages to choose action, but simply to warn them of the Romans' arrival.

אָמַר רַבִּי אֶלְעָזָר בֶּן עֲזַרְיָה: הֲרֵי אֲנִי כְּבֶן שִׁבְעִים שָׁנָה, וְלֹא

זָכִיתִי שֶׁתֵּאָמֵר יְצִיאַת מִצְרַיִם בַּלֵּילוֹת עַד שֶׁדְּרָשָׁהּ בֶּן זוֹמָא,

שֶׁנֶּאֱמַר: לְמַעַן תִּזְכֹּר אֶת יוֹם צֵאתְךָ מֵאֶרֶץ מִצְרַיִם כֹּל יְמֵי

חַיֶּיךָ. יְמֵי חַיֶּיךָ הַיָּמִים; כֹּל יְמֵי חַיֶּיךָ הַלֵּילוֹת. וַחֲכָמִים אוֹמְרִים: יְמֵי חַיֶּיךָ הָעוֹלָם הַזֶּה; כֹּל יְמֵי חַיֶּיךָ לְהָבִיא לִימוֹת הַמָּשִׁיחַ.

Rabbi Elazar ben Azariah said: "I seem like a man of seventy, yet I never found an adequate explanation for why the story of the Exodus should be recited at night, until Ben Zoma interpreted the following verse, 'That you may remember the day when you came out of the land of Egypt all the days of your life.' Had the Torah mentioned only 'the days of your life' it would have meant the days only, but *all* the days of your life' means the nights as well. Other sages explained this verse differently: Had it been written 'the days of your life' it would have referred only to the world in which we live now. '*All* the days of your life' means the days of the Messianic era as well."

Rabbi Elazar ben Azariah was barely eighteen when, during an upheaval within the Academy, he was elected president. Upon hearing the news, he told the emissary, "I'm sorry, I cannot give you an immediate answer, I have to ask my wife." Her advice was to refuse the offer. "Where is the guarantee that those who unseated your predecessors would not do the same to you?" she said. "People appreciate a bottle of wine while there is wine in it. After they drink the wine, they throw the bottle away." But the young scholar did not heed his wife's advice. Instead, he asked: "Should one not drink wine simply because one day the bottle will be thrown away?" Legend tells us that in order to make Elazar ben Azariah's peers respect him more, God turned his beard white overnight. And this is why it is written in the Haggadah that Rabbi Elazar ben Azariah seemed "like a man of seventy." Other commentators claim it was the other way around: His responsibilities as president had aged him prematurely.

בָּרוּךְ הַמָּקוֹם, בָּרוּךְ הוּא. בָּרוּךְ שֶׁנָּתַן תּוֹרָה לְעַמּוֹ יִשְׂרָאֵל, בָּרוּךְ הוּא.

כְּנֶגֶד אַרְבָּעָה בָנִים דִּבְּרָה תוֹרָה: אֶחָד חָכָם, וְאֶחָד רָשָׁע, וְאֶחָד תָּם, וְאֶחָד שֶׁאֵינוֹ יוֹדֵעַ לִשְׁאוֹל.

Blessed be the Almighty whose presence is everywhere. Blessed be He. Blessed be He who gave the Torah to the people of Israel. Blessed be He.

The Torah speaks of four sons. One is wise, one is wicked, one is simple, and one does not know how to ask the question.

חָכָם מַה הוּא אוֹמֵר: מָה הָעֵדֹת וְהַחֻקִּים וְהַמִּשְׁפָּטִים אֲשֶׁר צִוָּה יְיָ אֱלֹהֵינוּ אֶתְכֶם? וְאַף אַתָּה אֱמָר לוֹ כְּהִלְכוֹת הַפֶּסַח, אֵין מַפְטִירִין אַחַר הַפֶּסַח אֲפִיקוֹמָן.

What does the wise son say? "All these testimonies, laws, and rulings given to us by God, what do they mean?" And so you teach your wise son all the laws of Passover, including the ruling that nothing should be eaten after the afikoman.

רָשָׁע מַה הוּא אוֹמֵר: מָה הָעֲבֹדָה הַזֹּאת לָכֶם? לָכֶם וְלֹא לוֹ. וּלְפִי שֶׁהוֹצִיא אֶת עַצְמוֹ מִן הַכְּלָל כָּפַר בָּעִקָּר. וְאַף אַתָּה הַקְהֵה אֶת שִׁנָּיו, וֶאֱמָר לוֹ: בַּעֲבוּר זֶה עָשָׂה יְיָ לִי בְּצֵאתִי מִמִּצְרָיִם. לִי וְלֹא לוֹ. אִלּוּ הָיָה שָׁם לֹא הָיָה נִגְאָל.

What does the wicked son say? "What does all this mean to you?" And because he says "to you" and not to himself, he removes himself from the community, and in so doing he denies God. And therefore, in return, you must make him feel uncomfortable and say, "It is because of that which God did for me when I came out of Egypt." "For me" and not for him. Had the wicked son been there, he would not have been redeemed.

תָּם מַה הוּא אוֹמֵר: מַה זֹּאת? וְאָמַרְתָּ אֵלָיו: בְּחֹזֶק יָד הוֹצִיאָנוּ יְיָ מִמִּצְרַיִם, מִבֵּית עֲבָדִים.

What does the simple son say? That son says, "What does all this mean?" And you answer, "With a mighty hand God freed the Jewish people from Egypt, from the house of bondage."

וְשֶׁאֵינוֹ יוֹדֵעַ לִשְׁאוֹל, אַתְּ פְּתַח לוֹ, שֶׁנֶּאֱמַר: וְהִגַּדְתָּ לְבִנְךָ בַּיּוֹם הַהוּא לֵאמֹר: בַּעֲבוּר זֶה עָשָׂה יְיָ לִי בְּצֵאתִי מִמִּצְרָיִם.

And what about the son who does not even know how to ask the question? You begin by quoting from the Torah, "And you shall tell your son on that day, 'We do all this because of that which God did for me when I came out of Egypt.'"

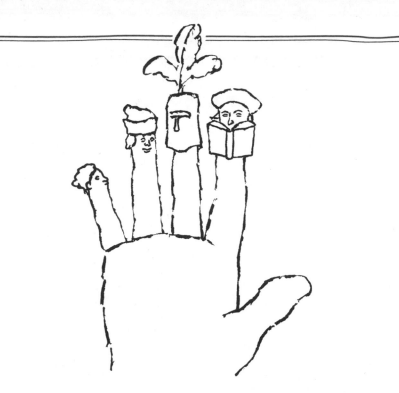

For Rabbi Samson Raphael Hirsch, the Orthodox scholar from Germany, the four sons symbolize four generations. The first follows the precepts of the father, the second rebels against them, the third submits without understanding them. As for the last, he doesn't even know that he doesn't know. In other words, there is regression and loss. The more removed each generation is from Sinai, the less it knows, the more complacent it becomes.

Actually, in Egypt the Jews *were* complacent. The pain and torment of persecutions had become familiar. A Midrash tells us that it took Pharaoh to chase them out of the country and force them to choose freedom.

The wicked son is guilty of more than complacency. He is condemned for being insolent. In the text the expression "Kofer b'ikar" stands out; it means someone who denies the essential, that is, someone who denies the existence of God. A "Kofer b'ikar" is not someone who opposes God, but someone who humiliates another human being. The wicked son has not insulted God; by remaining aloof, he has offended his fellow man.

Every year, when he reached this place in the text, the celebrated Rabbi Levi Yitzhak of Berditchev would stop to meditate. After a long silence, he would cry out, "God of Abraham, Isaac, and Jacob, the fourth son who does not even know how to ask the question, that is me, Levi Yitzhak. If I knew how to ask questions, I would ask You these questions: Read them in my heart, Almighty God, they are waiting for You there. I do not know why we suffer and endure all the exiles in the world. Nor do I know why our enemies are so powerful and why we are so weak. But doesn't the Haggadah tell us that it is up to the father to answer the fourth son, even though the fourth son does not ask the question? God of Abraham, Isaac, and Jacob, I am Your son. I am not asking You to reveal to me the secrets of Creation, or the mysteries of deliverance. Nor do I ask You to tell me the secret of Your presence in this world. I am asking You much less. Only that You tell me the meaning of my suffering. Tell me why we are persecuted so often, by so many, and please reassure me, at least by telling me that all that I suffer is for Your sake."

Interestingly, it is thanks to the fourth child that we are reading the most important verse of the Seder: "And you shall tell your son on that day . . ." This is the essence of our tradition. What is the meaning of tradition? The Hebrew *masorah* comes from the word *limsor*—to communicate. A Jew must communicate a tradition. Not to do so is to mutilate it. As a Jew it is my duty to tell my child not only my story, but also the story of my story, which is also my child's story. . . .

יָכוֹל מֵראשׁ חֹדֶשׁ, תַּלְמוּד לוֹמַר: בַּיוֹם הַהוּא.

אִי בַּיוֹם הַהוּא, יָכֹל מִבְּעוֹד יוֹם, תַּלְמוּד

לוֹמַר: בַּעֲבוּר זֶה. בַּעֲבוּר זֶה לֹא אָמַרְתִּי אֶלָּא בְּשָׁעָה שֶׁיֵּשׁ

מַצָּה וּמָרוֹר מֻנָּחִים לְפָנֶיךָ.

When do we begin telling the story? The Bible says, "And you shall tell your son on that day," meaning on the first day of Passover. Since the verse says "on that day" we might think that we should begin telling the story while it is still daytime. But the verse continues, "It is because of that which God did for me when I came out of Egypt." We can only say "because of that" when we are able to point to something that is symbolic of our suffering. So we tell the story when the unleavened bread and bitter herbs are set before us.

מִתְּחִלָּה עוֹבְדֵי עֲבוֹדָה זָרָה הָיוּ אֲבוֹתֵינוּ,

וְעַכְשָׁו קֵרְבָנוּ הַמָּקוֹם לַעֲבוֹדָתוֹ,

שֶׁנֶּאֱמַר: וַיֹּאמֶר יְהוֹשֻׁעַ אֶל כָּל הָעָם, כֹּה אָמַר יְיָ אֱלֹהֵי

יִשְׂרָאֵל: בְּעֵבֶר הַנָּהָר יָשְׁבוּ אֲבוֹתֵיכֶם מֵעוֹלָם, תֶּרַח אֲבִי

אַבְרָהָם וַאֲבִי נָחוֹר; וַיַּעַבְדוּ אֱלֹהִים אֲחֵרִים. וָאֶקַּח אֶת אֲבִיכֶם

אֶת אַבְרָהָם מֵעֵבֶר הַנָּהָר, וָאוֹלֵךְ אוֹתוֹ בְּכָל אֶרֶץ כְּנָעַן;

וָאַרְבֶּה אֶת זַרְעוֹ, וָאֶתֶּן לוֹ אֶת יִצְחָק. וָאֶתֵּן לְיִצְחָק אֶת יַעֲקֹב

וְאֶת עֵשָׂו; וָאֶתֵּן לְעֵשָׂו אֶת הַר שֵׂעִיר לָרֶשֶׁת אוֹתוֹ, וְיַעֲקֹב

וּבָנָיו יָרְדוּ מִצְרָיִם.

In the beginning, our forefathers were idol worshipers. But now the Lord is our God and we worship only Him, as it is written in the Bible, "Then Joshua spoke to all the people, 'This is what the Lord, the God of Israel has said: Long ago your ancestors, including Terach, father of Abraham and Nachor, lived beyond the River

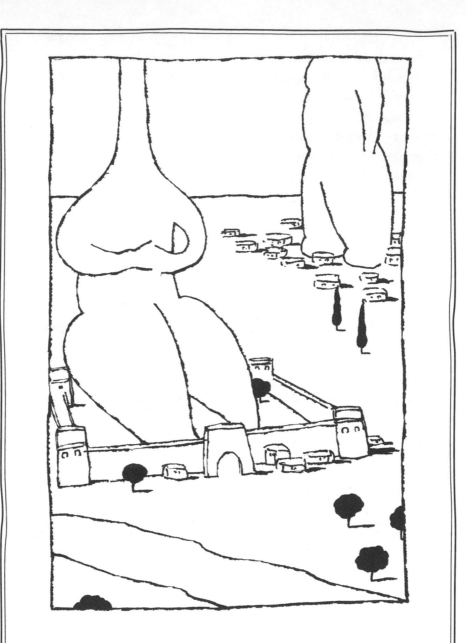

Euphrates and worshiped idols. But I took your father, Abraham, from beyond the river and led him through the entire land of Canaan and I multiplied his offspring. I gave him Isaac. And to Isaac I gave Jacob and Esau. I gave Esau Mount Seir as his possession; but Jacob and his children went down to Egypt.' "

Why does the text send us so far back in time? Is this the moment to remind us of the shortsightedness of our ancestors? Does the history of Israel begin before Israel? We are told that all men have the same beginning, that all our roots are buried in the same memory. And that innocence and guilt are not collective, nor are they hereditary; the most wicked of men may give life to the most righteous of men. Talmudic legend tells us that Nero converted, and that among his descendants there was a great scholar, a very great spiritual master. Never mind that our ancestors were pagans; we are judged not by what they were, but by what we are today.

בָּרוּךְ שׁוֹמֵר הַבְטָחָתוֹ לְיִשְׂרָאֵל, בָּרוּךְ הוּא.
שֶׁהַקָּדוֹשׁ בָּרוּךְ הוּא חִשַּׁב אֶת הַקֵּץ
לַעֲשׂוֹת כְּמוֹ שֶׁאָמַר לְאַבְרָהָם אָבִינוּ בִּבְרִית בֵּין הַבְּתָרִים,
שֶׁנֶּאֱמַר: וַיֹּאמֶר לְאַבְרָם, יָדֹעַ תֵּדַע כִּי גֵר יִהְיֶה זַרְעֲךָ בְּאֶרֶץ
לֹא לָהֶם, וַעֲבָדוּם וְעִנּוּ אֹתָם, אַרְבַּע מֵאוֹת שָׁנָה. וְגַם אֶת
הַגּוֹי אֲשֶׁר יַעֲבֹדוּ דָּן אָנֹכִי; וְאַחֲרֵי כֵן יֵצְאוּ בִּרְכֻשׁ גָּדוֹל.

Blessed be He who keeps His promise to Israel. Blessed be He. For God foresaw the end of bondage when He made His covenant with Abraham: "And God said to Abram: 'Know that your children and their children will be strangers in a strange land not their own. They shall be enslaved and oppressed for four hundred years. But also know that I will judge the nation that enslaved them. And in the end your children shall go free with great riches.' "

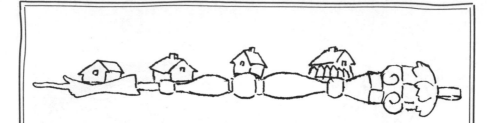

"Blessed be God who keeps His promise to Israel." The verb used, *shomer* (keeps), is in the present tense. Why? First, because for God, everything is in the present. And also because we deal here with a promise which renews itself every day. The divine promise made to Abraham, Isaac, and Jacob is also our promise, as though God had made this promise to every one of us. God promised *I* would return to Jerusalem. God promised *me* redemption.

"They shall be enslaved." The Talmud asks in astonishment: What did Pharaoh do to deserve the right to reduce Jews to slavery? And the Talmud answers: It is because Pharaoh was polite. When Abraham left Egypt, Pharaoh escorted him outside: "Because of the four steps that Pharaoh took that day, the descendants of Abraham will be enslaved to him for two hundred and ten years." Note that the Egyptian exile was intended to last four hundred years, a hundred years for each step. Then why was the sentence reduced? The Talmud tells us that Pharaoh issued the order to seize all male infants and bury them alive inside the pyramids. And God remained silent. The desperate parents cursed themselves for having brought children into the world. And God remained silent. Then one day the Angel Gabriel seized a newborn infant, one that had been maimed, and held him up to God. Only then did He remember the pledge made to Abraham, and set in motion the events which resulted in the Exodus. For God could not tolerate the sight of a mutilated Jewish child. Today our readers may well ask: If God and the Angel Gabriel felt sorry for one Jewish child in Egypt, where were they during the Night of Torment, when more than one million Jewish children were doomed to suffer and die?

וְהִיא שֶׁעָמְדָה לַאֲבוֹתֵינוּ וְלָנוּ, שֶׁלֹּא אֶחָד בִּלְבָד עָמַד עָלֵינוּ לְכַלּוֹתֵנוּ, אֶלָּא שֶׁבְּכָל דּוֹר וָדוֹר עוֹמְדִים עָלֵינוּ לְכַלּוֹתֵנוּ, וְהַקָּדוֹשׁ בָּרוּךְ הוּא מַצִּילֵנוּ מִיָּדָם.

This is the promise which has sustained our forefathers and ourselves. For it was not one man alone who rose against us to destroy us. In every generation they rise up to destroy us. And God, blessed be He, saves us from their hands.

We put our cups down and uncover the matzot.

While the Haggadah tells us that God saves us from the enemy, our history tells us otherwise.

Our enemies are frequently remembered only for the evil they have inflicted upon us. Were it not for us, who would remember Antiochus? Who would remember Titus? Or Haman? Is that why they hate and harm us, in order to be remembered by us and through us? It would seem that they wish to be part of our memory at any cost; anything is better than oblivion. The fact is that we have survived and so has our memory.

Surely, the Haggadah may be seen as a tale of Jewish survival.

צֵא וּלְמַד מַה בִּקֵּשׁ לָבָן הָאֲרַמִּי לַעֲשׂוֹת לְיַעֲקֹב אָבִינוּ. שֶׁפַּרְעֹה לֹא גָזַר אֶלָּא עַל הַזְּכָרִים, וְלָבָן בִּקֵּשׁ לַעֲקוֹר אֶת

הַכֹּל, שֶׁנֶּאֱמַר: אֲרַמִּי אֹבֵד אָבִי, וַיֵּרֶד מִצְרַיְמָה, וַיָּגָר שָׁם בִּמְתֵי מְעָט; וַיְהִי שָׁם לְגוֹי גָּדוֹל עָצוּם וָרָב.

Go learn and see what Laban the Aramaean tried to do to Jacob, our father. While Pharaoh decreed death only for male children, Laban thought to eradicate us all. As it is said: "An Aramaean attempted to destroy my father. Then he went down into Egypt and dwelled there, with few people. And there he became a nation, great, mighty, and numerous."

God saved our people not only from the hands of Pharaoh, but also from those of Laban. Laban does not fare well in the Haggadah, which says that he was worse than Pharaoh. He was a member of Isaac's family; thus one would surely expect more compassion. Laban did everything in his power to prevent Jacob from marrying his daughter, says the Talmud. He even tried to poison Abraham's servant, the matchmaker Eliezer, when he came to provide a bride for Isaac. Had he succeeded, there would have been no match, no sons, no future for Israel.

וַיֵּרֶד מִצְרַיְמָה, אָנוּס עַל פִּי הַדִּבּוּר.

וַיָּגָר שָׁם, מְלַמֵּד שֶׁלֹּא יָרַד יַעֲקֹב אָבִינוּ לְהִשְׁתַּקֵּעַ בְּמִצְרַיִם אֶלָּא לָגוּר שָׁם, שֶׁנֶּאֱמַר: וַיֹּאמְרוּ אֶל פַּרְעֹה, לָגוּר בָּאָרֶץ בָּאנוּ, כִּי אֵין מִרְעֶה לַצֹּאן אֲשֶׁר לַעֲבָדֶיךָ, כִּי כָבֵד הָרָעָב בְּאֶרֶץ כְּנָעַן; וְעַתָּה יֵשְׁבוּ נָא עֲבָדֶיךָ בְּאֶרֶץ גֹּשֶׁן.

"Then he went down into Egypt." What does this mean? It means that he was compelled by the word of God.

"And dwelled there." This means that Jacob did not go down into Egypt to settle, but to stay there for a while. As it is written, "And they said to Pharaoh: 'We have come to dwell in this land for there is no food for our flocks, since the famine is severe in the land of Canaan. We pray that you allow us to stay in the region of Goshen.' "

When God appeared to Jacob for the last time, He assuaged his fears: "I shall go with you to Egypt." Our ancient sages view this as a promise that the Shekhina, the Divine Presence, would follow Israel everywhere, even into exile; hence the certainty that Israel will never be abandoned and that Israel's redemption will bring about God's as well.

בִּמְתֵי מְעָט, כְּמוֹ שֶׁנֶּאֱמַר: בְּשִׁבְעִים נֶפֶשׁ יָרְדוּ אֲבֹתֶיךָ
מִצְרָיְמָה; וְעַתָּה שָׂמְךָ יְיָ אֱלֹהֶיךָ כְּכוֹכְבֵי הַשָּׁמַיִם לָרֹב.

וַיְהִי שָׁם לְגוֹי, מְלַמֵּד שֶׁהָיוּ יִשְׂרָאֵל מְצֻיָּנִים שָׁם.

גָּדוֹל עָצוּם, כְּמוֹ שֶׁנֶּאֱמַר: וּבְנֵי יִשְׂרָאֵל פָּרוּ וַיִּשְׁרְצוּ, וַיִּרְבּוּ
וַיַּעַצְמוּ בִּמְאֹד מְאֹד; וַתִּמָּלֵא הָאָרֶץ אֹתָם.

וָרָב, כְּמוֹ שֶׁנֶּאֱמַר: רְבָבָה כְּצֶמַח הַשָּׂדֶה נְתַתִּיךְ, וַתִּרְבִּי
וַתִּגְדְּלִי, וַתָּבֹאִי בַּעֲדִי עֲדָיִים; שָׁדַיִם נָכֹנוּ, וּשְׂעָרֵךְ צִמֵּחַ, וְאַתְּ
עֵרֹם וְעֶרְיָה.

"With few people." This means that "Your forefathers went down into Egypt with seventy persons. And now God has made you as numerous as the stars in heaven."

"And there he became a nation." This means that in Egypt, Israel became a separate nation, a nation unto itself.

"Great and mighty." This refers to the Biblical verse: "And the Children of Israel were fruitful and multiplied and grew strong and numerous and the land was filled with them."

"And numerous." This refers to the Biblical verse: "I let you multiply like the plants of the field and you have become numerous and grown strong, and you have attained excellence and beauty. You are now fully grown, yet you remain naked and bare."

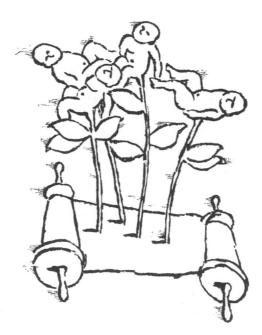

When Jacob's children first settled in Egypt, they were prosperous, respected, and content. But soon people began to envy them, and then to fear them, and eventually to hate them. They were thought to be too rich. Too numerous. Too powerful. Yet, when the Egyptians became embroiled in a bloody war with their neigh-

bors, they owed their eventual salvation to Jewish intervention. That was when the danger that hung over the Children of Israel became real. For to be indebted to the Jews was something Egyptians could not tolerate. Still, as long as one child of Jacob was alive, nobody dared attack the Jewish tribes. Only with the death of Levi, the last surviving son, did conditions dramatically change. The first anti-Jewish measures were adopted, resulting in forced labor and public humiliations.

וָאֶעֱבֹר עָלַיִךְ וָאֶרְאֵךְ מִתְבּוֹסֶסֶת בְּדָמָיִךְ וָאֹמַר לָךְ בְּדָמַיִךְ חֲיִי,

וָאֹמַר לָךְ בְּדָמַיִךְ חֲיִי.

"When I passed over you and saw you wallowing in your blood, I said to you: 'Through your blood live!' I said to you: 'Through your blood live!'"

וַיָּרֵעוּ אֹתָנוּ הַמִּצְרִים וַיְעַנּוּנוּ, וַיִּתְּנוּ עָלֵינוּ עֲבֹדָה קָשָׁה.

וַיָּרֵעוּ אֹתָנוּ הַמִּצְרִים, כְּמוֹ שֶׁנֶּאֱמַר: הָבָה נִתְחַכְּמָה לוֹ, פֶּן יִרְבֶּה, וְהָיָה כִּי תִקְרֶאנָה מִלְחָמָה, וְנוֹסַף גַּם הוּא עַל שֹׂנְאֵינוּ וְנִלְחַם בָּנוּ וְעָלָה מִן הָאָרֶץ.

"The Egyptians dealt harshly with us and they made us suffer; and they forced upon us hard labor."

"The Egyptians dealt harshly with us." As it is written in the Bible: "Come, let us deal shrewdly with them so they do not grow larger in numbers. Otherwise, if war occurs, they will help our enemies and fight against us and leave our land."

וַיְעַנּוּנוּ כְּמוֹ שֶׁנֶּאֱמַר: וַיָּשִׂימוּ עָלָיו שָׂרֵי מִסִּים, לְמַעַן עַנֹּתוֹ בְּסִבְלֹתָם. וַיִּבֶן עָרֵי מִסְכְּנוֹת לְפַרְעֹה, אֶת פִּתֹם וְאֶת רַעַמְסֵס. וַיִּתְּנוּ עָלֵינוּ עֲבֹדָה קָשָׁה, כְּמוֹ שֶׁנֶּאֱמַר: וַיַּעֲבִדוּ מִצְרַיִם אֶת בְּנֵי יִשְׂרָאֵל בְּפָרֶךְ.

"And they made us suffer." As the Bible relates: "So the Egyptians set out in order to oppress them even more with a harsher burden. And they built for Pharaoh the treasure cities Pithom and Rameses."

"And they forced upon us hard labor." As the Bible says: "The Egyptians ruthlessly imposed upon the Children of Israel rigorous labors."

וַנִּצְעַק אֶל יְיָ אֱלֹהֵי אֲבֹתֵינוּ, וַיִּשְׁמַע יְיָ אֶת קֹלֵנוּ, וַיַּרְא אֶת עָנְיֵנוּ, וְאֶת עֲמָלֵנוּ, וְאֶת לַחֲצֵנוּ.

וַנִּצְעַק אֶל יְיָ אֱלֹהֵי אֲבֹתֵינוּ, כְּמוֹ שֶׁנֶּאֱמַר: וַיְהִי בַיָּמִים הָרַבִּים הָהֵם, וַיָּמָת מֶלֶךְ מִצְרַיִם, וַיֵּאָנְחוּ בְנֵי יִשְׂרָאֵל מִן הָעֲבֹדָה וַיִּזְעָקוּ; וַתַּעַל שַׁוְעָתָם אֶל הָאֱלֹהִים מִן הָעֲבֹדָה.

"We cried to the Lord, the God of our fathers, and the Lord heard our plea and saw our plight, our misery, and our oppression."

"We cried to the Lord." The Bible recounts: "And it came to pass that the King of Egypt died. And the Children of Israel sighed from their hard labor and cried out; and their cry for help rose up to God."

A commentary from the Rabbi of Kotzk: They sighed? Why did they sigh? They should have been happy. True, said the Rabbi of Kotzk, but until the King of Egypt died, they did not even have the right to sigh.

וַיִּשְׁמַע יְיָ אֶת קֹלֵנוּ, כְּמוֹ שֶׁנֶּאֱמַר: וַיִּשְׁמַע אֱלֹהִים אֶת נַאֲקָתָם, וַיִּזְכֹּר אֱלֹהִים אֶת בְּרִיתוֹ אֶת אַבְרָהָם, אֶת יִצְחָק וְאֶת יַעֲקֹב.

וַיַּרְא אֶת עָנְיֵנוּ, זוֹ פְּרִישׁוּת דֶּרֶךְ אֶרֶץ, כְּמוֹ שֶׁנֶּאֱמַר: וַיַּרְא אֱלֹהִים אֶת בְּנֵי יִשְׂרָאֵל, וַיֵּדַע אֱלֹהִים.

"And the Lord heard our plea." As the Bible tells us: "And God heard their moaning. And God remembered His covenant. He remembered Abraham. He remembered Isaac. He remembered Jacob."

"And saw our plight." This refers to the compulsory separation that Pharaoh imposed on husband and wife. As the Bible tells us: "And God saw the Children of Israel and God understood their plight."

According to our sages, this means He saw the threat to family life. Men worked at night and therefore could not be with their

wives, as they would no longer live under one roof. However, in Jewish tradition, the family is sacred, redeeming. The Jewish people would not have survived, were it not for its obsession with family.

וְאֶת עֲמָלֵנוּ, אֵלּוּ הַבָּנִים, כְּמוֹ שֶׁנֶּאֱמַר: כָּל הַבֵּן הַיִּלּוֹד הַיְאֹרָה תַּשְׁלִיכֻהוּ, וְכָל הַבַּת תְּחַיּוּן.

וְאֶת לַחֲצֵנוּ, זֶה הַדְּחַק, כְּמוֹ שֶׁנֶּאֱמַר: וְגַם רָאִיתִי אֶת הַלַּחַץ אֲשֶׁר מִצְרַיִם לֹחֲצִים אֹתָם.

"Our misery." This refers to the drowning of the male children. As it is said: "Every son that is born shall be thrown into the Nile but every daughter may be kept alive."

"And our oppression." This speaks of the cruel crushing of our lives. As the Bible says: "I have seen how the Egyptians are oppressing them."

Strangely enough, Moses' name is mentioned only once in the Haggadah. But in the Midrash all credit is restored to him. We read of his encounter with the flaming bush, his solitude, his anguish as he heard the voice both distant and close, insistent, probing. How could any human being, even Moses, resist that voice? And yet it took God seven days to convince Moses to serve as His messenger. "Why me?" said Moses. "Why not an angel? Or my older brother Aaron? I am a poor speaker. And furthermore, what am I supposed to tell the Children of Israel when they question me?" And God said: "Tell them that I the Lord sent you and that I will be with them in their oppression in Egypt and I will be with them when other people enslave them." Whereupon Moses responded: "They have not even been freed from this enslavement, and yet shall I tell them of future enslavements?" And so God answered: "Tell them only that I the Lord sent you."

וַ"וֹ"צִ"אֵ"נּ"וֹ" יְיָ מִמִּצְרַיִם בְּיָד חֲזָקָה וּבִזְרֹעַ נְטוּיָה וּבְמֹרָא גָדֹל וּבְאֹתוֹת וּבְמֹפְתִים.

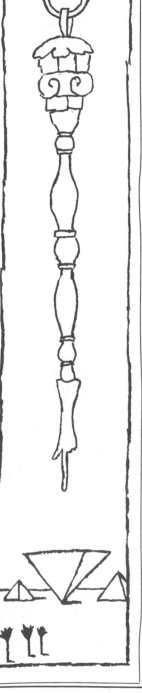

וַיּוֹצִיאֵנוּ יְיָ מִמִּצְרַיִם, לֹא עַל יְדֵי מַלְאָךְ, וְלֹא עַל יְדֵי שָׂרָף, וְלֹא עַל יְדֵי שָׁלִיחַ, אֶלָּא הַקָּדוֹשׁ בָּרוּךְ הוּא בִּכְבוֹדוֹ וּבְעַצְמוֹ, שֶׁנֶּאֱמַר: וְעָבַרְתִּי בְאֶרֶץ מִצְרַיִם בַּלַּיְלָה הַזֶּה, וְהִכֵּיתִי כָל בְּכוֹר בְּאֶרֶץ מִצְרַיִם, מֵאָדָם וְעַד בְּהֵמָה; וּבְכָל אֱלֹהֵי מִצְרַיִם אֶעֱשֶׂה שְׁפָטִים, אֲנִי יְיָ.

"And God pulled us out of Egypt with a mighty hand, and an outstretched arm, with great fear, and with signs and wonders."

"And God pulled us out of Egypt." The Holy One Himself brought us out of Egypt, not by an angel, not by an angel of fire, not even by the hands of a messenger. He Himself, He the glorious One, He the blessed One, brought us out of Egypt. As the Bible says: "And I will pass through the land of

Egypt on that night, and I will strike down all the firstborn men and beasts in the land of Egypt; and I will execute judgment against all the gods of Egypt, I the Lord."

וְעָבַרְתִּי בְאֶרֶץ מִצְרַיִם בַּלַּיְלָה הַזֶּה, אֲנִי וְלֹא מַלְאָךְ; וְהִכֵּיתִי כָל בְּכוֹר בְּאֶרֶץ מִצְרַיִם, אֲנִי וְלֹא שָׂרָף; וּבְכָל אֱלֹהֵי מִצְרַיִם אֶעֱשֶׂה שְׁפָטִים, אֲנִי וְלֹא הַשָּׁלִיחַ; אֲנִי יְיָ, אֲנִי הוּא וְלֹא אַחֵר.

"And I will pass through the land of Egypt," I, and not an angel. "And I will strike down the firstborn in the land of Egypt," I, and not an angel of fire. "And I will execute judgment against all the gods of Egypt," I, and not a messenger. "I the Lord, I, and not another."

What a curious passage. Why does God boast of killing innocent children, be they Egyptian? Why does He mention it so often? Is He proud of it? One may study Midrashic and Talmudic sources in search of an explanation. In vain. And yet there must be one. Is He teaching us an essential lesson? That He alone may kill? And that no one has the right to imitate Him?

בְּיָד חֲזָקָה, זוֹ הַדֶּבֶר, כְּמוֹ שֶׁנֶּאֱמַר: הִנֵּה יַד יְיָ הוֹיָה בְּמִקְנְךָ אֲשֶׁר בַּשָּׂדֶה, בַּסּוּסִים, בַּחֲמֹרִים, בַּגְּמַלִּים, בַּבָּקָר וּבַצֹּאן, דֶּבֶר כָּבֵד מְאֹד.

וּבִזְרֹעַ נְטוּיָה, זוֹ הַחֶרֶב, כְּמוֹ שֶׁנֶּאֱמַר: וְחַרְבּוֹ שְׁלוּפָה בְּיָדוֹ, נְטוּיָה עַל יְרוּשָׁלָיִם.

51

וּבְמֹרָא גָּדֹל, זֶה גִּלּוּי שְׁכִינָה, כְּמוֹ שֶׁנֶּאֱמַר: אוֹ הֲנִסָּה אֱלֹהִים לָבוֹא לָקַחַת לוֹ גוֹי מִקֶּרֶב גּוֹי בְּמַסֹּת, בְּאֹתֹת וּבְמוֹפְתִים וּבְמִלְחָמָה, וּבְיָד חֲזָקָה וּבִזְרוֹעַ נְטוּיָה, וּבְמוֹרָאִים גְּדֹלִים, כְּכֹל אֲשֶׁר עָשָׂה לָכֶם יְיָ אֱלֹהֵיכֶם בְּמִצְרַיִם לְעֵינֶיךָ.

"With a mighty hand." This refers to the pestilence. As the Bible says: "The hand of God will strike your livestock in the fields, the horses, the asses, the camels, the cattle, and the sheep, with a very severe pestilence."

"And an outstretched arm." This refers to the sword. As the Bible states: "His sword drawn in His hand outstretched over Jerusalem."

"With great fear." This refers to God's revelation of His presence to Israel. As it is said: "Has God ever tried to remove one nation from the midst of another nation, with trials, with upheavals, with signs, with wonders, with wars, and with a mighty hand and an outstretched arm, and with great fears and anguish, as the Lord your God did for you in Egypt before your very eyes?"

Why are we suddenly recalling Jerusalem? Because whenever we speak of exile, we remember Jerusalem. Jerusalem means redemption.

וּבְאֹתוֹת. זֶה הַמַּטֶּה, כְּמוֹ שֶׁנֶּאֱמַר: וְאֶת הַמַּטֶּה הַזֶּה תִּקַּח בְּיָדְךָ, אֲשֶׁר תַּעֲשֶׂה בּוֹ אֶת הָאֹתֹת.

וּבְמֹפְתִים, זֶה הַדָּם, כְּמוֹ שֶׁנֶּאֱמַר: וְנָתַתִּי מֹפְתִים בַּשָּׁמַיִם וּבָאָרֶץ:

"And with signs." This refers to the rod. As the Bible says: "Take this rod in your hand, and with it you shall perform miracles and signs."

"And wonders." This refers to the plague of blood. As the Bible says: "I will show wonders in heaven and on earth":

A drop of wine is removed from our cups as each wonder is recited.

דָּם, וָאֵשׁ, וְתִימְרוֹת עָשָׁן.

"BLOOD, FIRE, AND PILLARS OF SMOKE."

דָּבָר אַחֵר: בְּיָד חֲזָקָה שְׁתַּיִם; וּבִזְרֹעַ נְטוּיָה שְׁתַּיִם; וּבְמֹרָא

גָּדֹל שְׁתַּיִם; וּבְאֹתוֹת שְׁתַּיִם; וּבְמֹפְתִים שְׁתַּיִם.

There is another interpretation:
The words "mighty hand" represent two plagues.
The words "outstretched arm" represent another two.
"Great fear" signifies two more.
Then two for "signs," and
two for "wonders."

Why do we dip a finger in wine and spill a drop for each of the three wonders? To signify our compassion for the Egyptians who were also victims, albeit of their own arrogance. That is why we spill the three drops of wine, and then later, the ten drops, when we recite the ten plagues. Also, to manifest our sadness.

Our tradition prohibits us from celebrating the defeat of the enemy.

אֵלּוּ עֶשֶׂר מַכּוֹת, שֶׁהֵבִיא הַקָּדוֹשׁ בָּרוּךְ הוּא עַל הַמִּצְרִים

בְּמִצְרַיִם, וְאֵלּוּ הֵן:

These are the ten plagues that God, blessed be He, brought upon the Egyptians in Egypt:

A drop of wine is removed from our cups as each plague is recited.

דָּם. צְפַרְדֵּעַ. כִּנִּים. עָרוֹב. דֶּבֶר. שְׁחִין. בָּרָד. אַרְבֶּה. חֹשֶׁךְ. מַכַּת בְּכוֹרוֹת.

**BLOOD   FROGS   LICE
WILD BEASTS   PESTILENCE   BOILS
HAIL   LOCUSTS   DARKNESS
THE SLAYING OF THE FIRSTBORN**

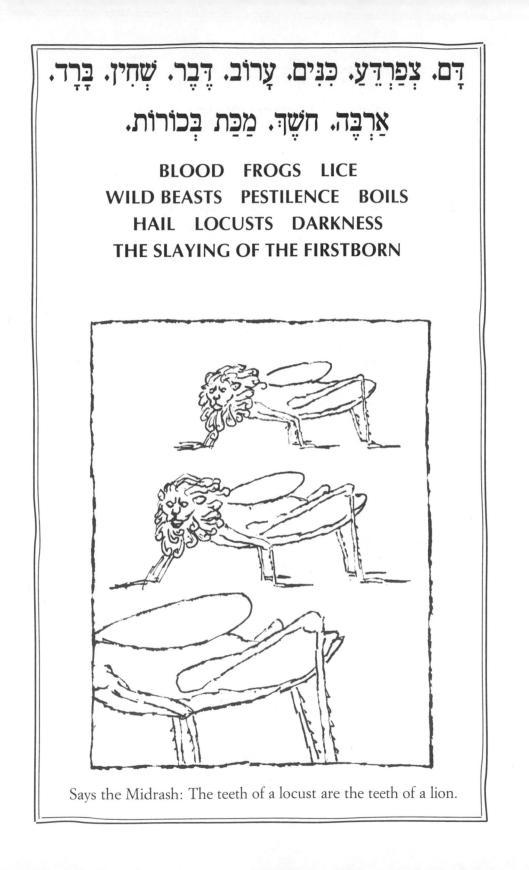

Says the Midrash: The teeth of a locust are the teeth of a lion.

רַבִּי יְהוּדָה הָיָה נוֹתֵן בָּהֶם סִימָנִים:

Rabbi Yehuda liked to refer to the ten plagues by their Hebrew initials:

דְּצַ"ךְ, עַדַ"שׁ, בְּאַחַ"ב.

DETZAKH   ADASH   BEACHAV

רַבִּי יוֹסֵי הַגְּלִילִי אוֹמֵר: מִנַּיִן אַתָּה אוֹמֵר שֶׁלָּקוּ הַמִּצְרִים בְּמִצְרַיִם עֶשֶׂר מַכּוֹת, וְעַל הַיָּם לָקוּ חֲמִשִּׁים מַכּוֹת. בְּמִצְרַיִם מַה הוּא אוֹמֵר: וַיֹּאמְרוּ הַחַרְטֻמִּם אֶל פַּרְעֹה, אֶצְבַּע אֱלֹהִים הִיא. וְעַל הַיָּם מַה הוּא אוֹמֵר: וַיַּרְא יִשְׂרָאֵל אֶת הַיָּד הַגְּדוֹלָה אֲשֶׁר עָשָׂה יְיָ

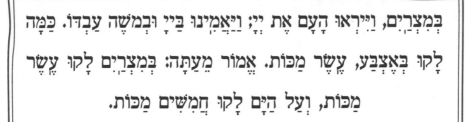

בְּמִצְרַיִם, וַיִּירְאוּ הָעָם אֶת יְיָ; וַיַּאֲמִינוּ בַּיְיָ וּבְמֹשֶׁה עַבְדּוֹ. כַּמָּה לָקוּ בְּאֶצְבַּע, עֶשֶׂר מַכּוֹת. אֱמוֹר מֵעַתָּה: בְּמִצְרַיִם לָקוּ עֶשֶׂר מַכּוֹת, וְעַל הַיָּם לָקוּ חֲמִשִּׁים מַכּוֹת.

Rabbi Yossé of Galilee said: "How do we know that the Egyptians were punished in Egypt with ten plagues and at the Red Sea with fifty? According to the Bible, the magicians in Egypt told Pharaoh that they saw the finger of God in the plagues. While this is what the Bible says about the Red Sea: 'And when Israel saw the mighty hand which God had wielded against Egypt, the people revered God and believed in God.' If one finger of God in Egypt caused ten plagues, we may properly assume that the whole hand of God at the Red Sea caused fifty plagues."

רַבִּי אֱלִיעֶזֶר אוֹמֵר: מִנַּיִן שֶׁכָּל מַכָּה וּמַכָּה, שֶׁהֵבִיא הַקָּדוֹשׁ בָּרוּךְ הוּא עַל הַמִּצְרִים בְּמִצְרַיִם, הָיְתָה שֶׁל אַרְבַּע מַכּוֹת, שֶׁנֶּאֱמַר: יְשַׁלַּח בָּם חֲרוֹן אַפּוֹ, עֶבְרָה, וָזַעַם, וְצָרָה, מִשְׁלַחַת מַלְאֲכֵי רָעִים. עֶבְרָה אַחַת, וָזַעַם שְׁתַּיִם, וְצָרָה שָׁלֹשׁ, מִשְׁלַחַת מַלְאֲכֵי רָעִים אַרְבַּע. אֱמוֹר מֵעַתָּה: בְּמִצְרַיִם לָקוּ אַרְבָּעִים מַכּוֹת, וְעַל הַיָּם לָקוּ מָאתַיִם מַכּוֹת.

Rabbi Eliezer said: "How do we know that every plague which God, blessed be He, inflicted upon the Egyptians in Egypt actually consisted of four plagues? Because it is said in the Book of Psalms: 'He sent against the Egyptians His fiery anger: wrath, indignation,

trouble, and the messengers of evil.' So we may interpret that 'wrath' implies one; 'indignation,' two; 'trouble,' three; and 'the messengers of evil,' four. If in Egypt they were punished with forty plagues, then at the Red Sea they suffered two hundred plagues.''

רַבִּי עֲקִיבָא אוֹמֵר: מִנַּיִן שֶׁכָּל מַכָּה וּמַכָּה, שֶׁהֵבִיא הַקָּדוֹשׁ בָּרוּךְ הוּא עַל הַמִּצְרִים בְּמִצְרַיִם הָיְתָה שֶׁל חָמֵשׁ מַכּוֹת, שֶׁנֶּאֱמַר: יְשַׁלַּח בָּם חֲרוֹן אַפּוֹ, עֶבְרָה, וָזַעַם, וְצָרָה, מִשְׁלַחַת מַלְאֲכֵי רָעִים. חֲרוֹן אַפּוֹ אַחַת, עֶבְרָה שְׁתַּיִם, וָזַעַם שָׁלֹשׁ, וְצָרָה אַרְבַּע, מִשְׁלַחַת מַלְאֲכֵי רָעִים חָמֵשׁ. אֱמוֹר מֵעַתָּה: בְּמִצְרַיִם לָקוּ חֲמִשִּׁים מַכּוֹת, וְעַל הַיָּם לָקוּ חֲמִשִּׁים וּמָאתַיִם מַכּוֹת.

Rabbi Akiba said: ''Similarly, we may say, that every plague which God, blessed be He, inflicted upon the Egyptians in Egypt actually consisted of five plagues. The verse states: 'He sent against the Egyptians His fiery anger, wrath, indignation, trouble, and the messengers of evil.' Thus, each plague was inflicted with 'His fiery anger,' one; 'wrath,' two; 'indignation,' three; 'trouble,' four; and 'the messengers of evil,' five. And so, if in Egypt they were stricken with fifty plagues, at the Red Sea they suffered no less than two hundred and fifty plagues.''

Why this discussion? Does it indicate a spirit of vindictiveness on the part of our sages? Or were they simply emphasizing the love that the God of Israel showed His people by punishing their

enemies? Thus are we to conclude that the more He punished the Egyptians, the more He loved their victims? Or as the Gaon of Vilna explained, the sages multiplied the plagues in accordance with the Biblical verse: "All the afflictions I brought upon the Egyptians I will not bring upon you." According to the Gaon, the more plagues inflicted upon the Egyptians, the less to befall the Children of Israel.

כַּמָּה מַעֲלוֹת טוֹבוֹת לַמָּקוֹם עָלֵינוּ:

אִלּוּ הוֹצִיאָנוּ מִמִּצְרַיִם, וְלֹא עָשָׂה בָהֶם שְׁפָטִים,   דַּיֵּנוּ.

אִלּוּ עָשָׂה בָהֶם שְׁפָטִים, וְלֹא עָשָׂה בֵאלֹהֵיהֶם,   דַּיֵּנוּ.

אִלּוּ עָשָׂה בֵאלֹהֵיהֶם, וְלֹא הָרַג אֶת בְּכוֹרֵיהֶם,   דַּיֵּנוּ.

אִלּוּ הָרַג אֶת בְּכוֹרֵיהֶם, וְלֹא נָתַן לָנוּ אֶת מָמוֹנָם,   דַּיֵּנוּ.

אִלּוּ נָתַן לָנוּ אֶת מָמוֹנָם, וְלֹא קָרַע לָנוּ אֶת הַיָּם,   דַּיֵּנוּ.

אִלּוּ קָרַע לָנוּ אֶת הַיָּם, וְלֹא הֶעֱבִירָנוּ בְּתוֹכוֹ

בֶּחָרָבָה,   דַּיֵּנוּ.

אִלּוּ הֶעֱבִירָנוּ בְּתוֹכוֹ בֶּחָרָבָה, וְלֹא שִׁקַּע צָרֵינוּ

בְּתוֹכוֹ,   דַּיֵּנוּ.

אִלּוּ שִׁקַּע צָרֵינוּ בְּתוֹכוֹ, וְלֹא סִפֵּק צָרְכֵּנוּ

בַּמִּדְבָּר אַרְבָּעִים שָׁנָה,   דַּיֵּנוּ.

אִלּוּ סִפֵּק צָרְכֵּנוּ בַּמִּדְבָּר אַרְבָּעִים שָׁנָה, וְלֹא

הֶאֱכִילָנוּ אֶת הַמָּן,　דַּיֵּנוּ.

אִלּוּ הֶאֱכִילָנוּ אֶת הַמָּן, וְלֹא נָתַן לָנוּ אֶת הַשַּׁבָּת,　דַּיֵּנוּ.

אִלּוּ נָתַן לָנוּ אֶת הַשַּׁבָּת, וְלֹא קֵרְבָנוּ לִפְנֵי הַר סִינַי,　דַּיֵּנוּ.

אִלּוּ קֵרְבָנוּ לִפְנֵי הַר סִינַי, וְלֹא נָתַן לָנוּ אֶת הַתּוֹרָה,　דַּיֵּנוּ.

אִלּוּ נָתַן לָנוּ אֶת הַתּוֹרָה וְלֹא הִכְנִיסָנוּ לְאֶרֶץ יִשְׂרָאֵל,　דַּיֵּנוּ.

אִלּוּ הִכְנִיסָנוּ לְאֶרֶץ יִשְׂרָאֵל, וְלֹא בָנָה לָנוּ אֶת

בֵּית הַבְּחִירָה,　דַּיֵּנוּ.

Dayenu

How thankful and grateful must we be to God for all the marvelous
　things He did for us.
Had He delivered us from Egypt and not punished the Egyptians,
　it would have sufficed.

Had He punished the Egyptians and not destroyed their idols, it would have sufficed.

Had He destroyed their idols and not slain their firstborn, it would have sufficed.

Had He slain their firstborn and not given us their fortunes, it would have sufficed.

Had He given us their fortunes and not parted the sea for us, it would have sufficed.

Had He parted the sea for us and not brought us through the sea on dry land, it would have sufficed.

Had He brought us through the sea on dry land and not drowned our oppressors in the sea, it would have sufficed.

Had He drowned our oppressors in the sea and not helped us for forty years in the desert, it would have sufficed.

Had He helped us for forty years in the desert and not fed us manna, it would have sufficed.

Had He fed us manna and not given us the Sabbath, it would have sufficed.

Had He given us the Sabbath and not brought us to Mount Sinai, it would have sufficed.

Had He brought us to Mount Sinai and not given us the Torah, it would have sufficed.

Had He given us the Torah and not brought us into the land of Israel, it would have sufficed.

Had he brought us into the land of Israel and not built for us the Temple, the Holy Temple, it would still have sufficed.

The name of this beautiful prayer is *Dayenu*, which means "it would have sufficed" or "we would have been satisfied." Perhaps "grateful" would be a better translation. *Dayenu* is the song of our gratitude. A Jew defines himself by his capacity for gratitude. A Jewish philosopher was once asked, "What is the opposite of nihilism?" And he said, *"Dayenu,"* the ability to be thankful for what we have received, for what we are. The first prayer a Jew is

expected to recite upon waking expresses his gratitude for being alive. This holds for all generations, and surely for ours. For each of us, every day should be an act of grace, every hour a miraculous offering.

עַל אַחַת כַּמָּה וְכַמָּה טוֹבָה כְפוּלָה וּמְכֻפֶּלֶת לַמָּקוֹם עָלֵינוּ:

שֶׁהוֹצִיאָנוּ מִמִּצְרַיִם, וְעָשָׂה בָהֶם שְׁפָטִים, וְעָשָׂה בֵאלֹהֵיהֶם,

וְהָרַג אֶת בְּכוֹרֵיהֶם, וְנָתַן לָנוּ אֶת מָמוֹנָם, וְקָרַע לָנוּ אֶת הַיָּם,

וְהֶעֱבִירָנוּ בְּתוֹכוֹ בֶּחָרָבָה, וְשִׁקַּע צָרֵינוּ בְּתוֹכוֹ, וְסִפֵּק צָרְכֵּנוּ

בַּמִּדְבָּר אַרְבָּעִים שָׁנָה, וְהֶאֱכִילָנוּ אֶת הַמָּן, וְנָתַן לָנוּ אֶת

הַשַּׁבָּת, וְקֵרְבָנוּ לִפְנֵי הַר סִינַי, וְנָתַן לָנוּ אֶת הַתּוֹרָה,

וְהִכְנִיסָנוּ לְאֶרֶץ יִשְׂרָאֵל, וּבָנָה לָנוּ אֶת בֵּית הַבְּחִירָה לְכַפֵּר

עַל כָּל עֲוֹנוֹתֵינוּ.

Then how much more grateful are we for the countless blessings of God given to us, then and now: That He delivered us from Egypt, and punished the Egyptians, and destroyed their idols, and slew their firstborn, and gave us their fortunes, and parted the sea for us, and brought us through the sea on dry land, and drowned our oppressors in the sea, and helped us for forty years in the desert, and fed us manna, and gave us the Sabbath, and brought us to Mount Sinai, and gave us the Torah, and brought us into the land of Israel, and built for us the Holy Temple where we could atone for all our sins forever and ever.

רַבָּן גַּמְלִיאֵל הָיָה אוֹמֵר: כָּל שֶׁלֹּא אָמַר שְׁלוֹשָׁה דְבָרִים אֵלּוּ בַּפֶּסַח, לֹא יָצָא יְדֵי חוֹבָתוֹ, וְאֵלּוּ הֵן:

Rabbi Gamaliel would say, "Whoever does not discuss the meaning of the following three symbols of the Seder on Passover evening has not fulfilled his duty":

פֶּסַח, מַצָּה, וּמָרוֹר.

PESACH, MATZAH, AND MAROR

פֶּסַח שֶׁהָיוּ אֲבוֹתֵינוּ אוֹכְלִים בִּזְמַן שֶׁבֵּית הַמִּקְדָּשׁ קַיָּם, עַל שׁוּם מָה? עַל שׁוּם שֶׁפָּסַח הַקָּדוֹשׁ בָּרוּךְ הוּא עַל בָּתֵּי אֲבוֹתֵינוּ בְּמִצְרַיִם, שֶׁנֶּאֱמַר: וַאֲמַרְתֶּם זֶבַח פֶּסַח הוּא לַיָי, אֲשֶׁר פָּסַח עַל בָּתֵּי בְּנֵי יִשְׂרָאֵל בְּמִצְרַיִם, בְּנָגְפּוֹ אֶת מִצְרַיִם, וְאֶת בָּתֵּינוּ הִצִּיל. וַיִּקֹּד הָעָם וַיִּשְׁתַּחֲווּ.

A Midrashic saying: The Children of Israel called Pharaoh "Maror" because he embittered their lives.

Why Pesach? Why did our forefathers eat the Passover lamb in the days of the Holy Temple? They ate it so as to remember that God, blessed be He, passed over the houses of our ancestors in Egypt. As it is written in the Bible: "And you shall say it is the Passover sacrifice for God who passed over the houses of the Children of Israel in Egypt, when He killed the Egyptians and spared our houses. And the people bowed their heads in worship."

The head of the table lifts up or points to the matzah.

מַצָּה זוֹ, שֶׁאָנוּ אוֹכְלִים, עַל שׁוּם מָה? עַל שׁוּם שֶׁלֹּא הִסְפִּיק בְּצֵקָם שֶׁל אֲבוֹתֵינוּ לְהַחֲמִיץ עַד שֶׁנִּגְלָה עֲלֵיהֶם מֶלֶךְ מַלְכֵי הַמְּלָכִים, הַקָּדוֹשׁ בָּרוּךְ הוּא, וּגְאָלָם, שֶׁנֶּאֱמַר: וַיֹּאפוּ אֶת הַבָּצֵק אֲשֶׁר הוֹצִיאוּ מִמִּצְרַיִם, עֻגֹת מַצּוֹת כִּי לֹא חָמֵץ. כִּי גֹרְשׁוּ מִמִּצְרַיִם, וְלֹא יָכְלוּ לְהִתְמַהְמֵהַּ, וְגַם צֵדָה לֹא עָשׂוּ לָהֶם.

Why matzah? Why do we eat unleavened bread? Because there was not enough time for the dough made by our ancestors in Egypt to rise before the King of Kings, the Ruler of the Universe, blessed be He, chose to redeem them. As the Bible says: "And they baked the dough which they brought out of Egypt into unleavened cakes; it did not rise, because they were driven out of Egypt and could not delay; nor had they prepared any provisions for themselves."

מָרוֹר זֶה, שֶׁאָנוּ אוֹכְלִים, עַל שׁוּם מָה? עַל
שׁוּם שֶׁמֵּרֲרוּ הַמִּצְרִים אֶת חַיֵּי אֲבוֹתֵינוּ
בְּמִצְרָיִם, שֶׁנֶּאֱמַר: וַיְמָרֲרוּ אֶת חַיֵּיהֶם בַּעֲבֹדָה קָשָׁה, בְּחֹמֶר
וּבִלְבֵנִים, וּבְכָל עֲבֹדָה בַּשָּׂדֶה, אֶת כָּל עֲבֹדָתָם אֲשֶׁר עָבְדוּ
בָהֶם בְּפָרֶךְ.

Why maror? Why do we eat bitter herbs? They are eaten to remind us of how the Egyptians made the lives of our forefathers bitter. As it is written in the Bible: "And they embittered their lives with hard labor, with mortar and bricks, and with all sorts of work in the field, with all the tasks ruthlessly imposed upon them."

What does Rabbi Gamaliel tell us? That it is not enough to eat matzah and maror, nor to remember the Passover lamb. The words describing them must be said aloud, for all to hear. To listen to a story is no less important than to tell it. Sometimes it is even more important. "Sh'ma Israel," Listen O Israel. Is that not every Jew's declaration of faith? To listen is therefore the essence of the Passover commandment.

בְּכָל דּוֹר וָדוֹר חַיָּב אָדָם לִרְאוֹת אֶת עַצְמוֹ
כְּאִלּוּ הוּא יָצָא מִמִּצְרַיִם, שֶׁנֶּאֱמַר: וְהִגַּדְתָּ
לְבִנְךָ בַּיּוֹם הַהוּא לֵאמֹר: בַּעֲבוּר זֶה עָשָׂה יְיָ לִי בְּצֵאתִי

מִמִּצְרַיִם. לֹא אֶת אֲבוֹתֵינוּ בִּלְבַד גָּאַל הַקָּדוֹשׁ בָּרוּךְ הוּא,

אֶלָּא אַף אוֹתָנוּ גָּאַל עִמָּהֶם, שֶׁנֶּאֱמַר: וְאוֹתָנוּ הוֹצִיא מִשָּׁם,

לְמַעַן הָבִיא אֹתָנוּ, לָתֶת לָנוּ אֶת הָאָרֶץ אֲשֶׁר נִשְׁבַּע

לַאֲבֹתֵינוּ.

In every generation, every individual must feel as if he personally had come out of Egypt. As the Bible says: "And you shall tell your son on that day, 'It is because of that which God did for me when

I came out of Egypt.' " For it was not our ancestors alone whom God, blessed be He, redeemed. He redeemed all of us with them. As it is said: "He freed us from there that He might lead us to and give us the land which He promised our ancestors."

Two comments: First, the text does not say that every *Jew* must feel as if he had come out of Egypt. It says "every individual." And here we find the universal dimension of Jewish experience. After all, though the Torah was given to our people, have we not shared it with every other people? Second, the text says that every one of us must consider himself "as if" he had come out of Egypt. No, I did not leave Egypt, but I must think "as if" I had been among those who did. Certain Talmudic legends explain that actually our souls were there. Or we may accept the literal interpretation, and say: Though I have not personally taken part in those events, I must live "as if" I had. This lesson is especially relevant for those of our contemporaries who declare that all of us "are survivors of the Holocaust." No, all of us are not. Only those who went through the agony of Night survived that Night. Only those who knew death in Auschwitz survived Auschwitz. But all of us should think and act "as if" we had all been there. This "as if" defines the role of literature.

The matzot are covered, and we raise our cups of wine and say:

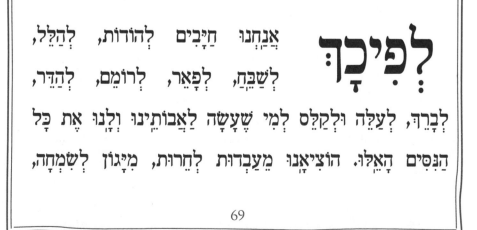

לְפִיכָך: אֲנַחְנוּ חַיָּבִים לְהוֹדוֹת, לְהַלֵּל,
לְשַׁבֵּחַ, לְפָאֵר, לְרוֹמֵם, לְהַדֵּר,
לְבָרֵך, לְעַלֵּה וּלְקַלֵּס לְמִי שֶׁעָשָׂה לַאֲבוֹתֵינוּ וְלָנוּ אֶת כָּל
הַנִּסִּים הָאֵלּוּ. הוֹצִיאָנוּ מֵעַבְדוּת לְחֵרוּת, מִיָּגוֹן לְשִׂמְחָה,

מֵאֵבֶל לְיוֹם טוֹב, וּמֵאֲפֵלָה לְאוֹר גָּדוֹל וּמִשַּׁעְבּוּד לִגְאֻלָּה.

וְנֹאמַר לְפָנָיו שִׁירָה חֲדָשָׁה; הַלְלוּיָהּ.

Therefore we must thank and praise, honor and glorify, exalt and acclaim, bless and adore God who performed all these wonders and miracles for our ancestors and for us. He brought us out of slavery to freedom. He changed anguish to joy, mourning to festivity, darkness to great light, and enslavement to redemption. Let us sing to Him and before Him a new song of praise: Halleluyah!

We put our cups down and the matzot are uncovered.

The celebrated Gaon of Vilna comments on this prayer: "The Haggadah uses nine different expressions to sing the praise of God, one for each of the first nine plagues. For the tenth, the slaying of the firstborn, we sing Hallel." According to the Kabbalah, this tenfold praise of God reflects the ten Sefirot, or emanations through which God governs the world.

הַלְלוּיָהּ הַלְלוּ, עַבְדֵי יְיָ, הַלְלוּ אֶת שֵׁם יְיָ.

יְהִי שֵׁם יְיָ מְבֹרָךְ, מֵעַתָּה וְעַד

עוֹלָם. מִמִּזְרַח שֶׁמֶשׁ עַד מְבוֹאוֹ, מְהֻלָּל שֵׁם יְיָ. רָם עַל כָּל

גּוֹיִם יְיָ, עַל הַשָּׁמַיִם כְּבוֹדוֹ. מִי כַּייָ אֱלֹהֵינוּ, הַמַּגְבִּיהִי לָשָׁבֶת.

הַמַּשְׁפִּילִי לִרְאוֹת בַּשָּׁמַיִם וּבָאָרֶץ. מְקִימִי מֵעָפָר דָּל, מֵאַשְׁפֹּת

יָרִים אֶבְיוֹן. לְהוֹשִׁיבִי עִם נְדִיבִים, עִם נְדִיבֵי עַמּוֹ. מוֹשִׁיבִי

עֲקֶרֶת הַבַּיִת, אֵם הַבָּנִים שְׂמֵחָה; הַלְלוּיָהּ.

Psalm 113

Halleluyah!
Servants of the Lord sing praise, praise the name of the Lord.
Blessed is the name of the Lord now and always.
From east to west the Lord's name is praised.
The Lord is supreme over all nations, His glory is beyond the
    heavens.
Who is like the Lord our God, enthroned on high,
    concerned with all below in heaven and on earth?
He raises the poor out of the dust, and the needy from humiliation,
    to seat them with nobility, with the most noble of His people.
And the barren woman, in her house, will become a happy mother
    of children.
Halleluyah!

71

בְּצֵאת יִשְׂרָאֵל מִמִּצְרָיִם, בֵּית יַעֲקֹב מֵעַם לֹעֵז. הָיְתָה יְהוּדָה לְקָדְשׁוֹ, יִשְׂרָאֵל מַמְשְׁלוֹתָיו. הַיָּם רָאָה וַיָּנֹס; הַיַּרְדֵּן יִסֹּב לְאָחוֹר. הֶהָרִים רָקְדוּ כְאֵילִים, גְּבָעוֹת כִּבְנֵי צֹאן. מַה לְּךָ, הַיָּם כִּי תָנוּס; הַיַּרְדֵּן, תִּסֹּב לְאָחוֹר. הֶהָרִים, תִּרְקְדוּ כְאֵילִים, גְּבָעוֹת, כִּבְנֵי צֹאן. מִלִּפְנֵי אָדוֹן חוּלִי אָרֶץ, מִלִּפְנֵי אֱלוֹהַּ יַעֲקֹב. הַהֹפְכִי הַצּוּר אֲגַם מָיִם, חַלָּמִישׁ לְמַעְיְנוֹ מָיִם.

Psalm 114

When Israel left Egypt, when the house of Jacob abandoned an
  alien tongue,
Judah became His sanctuary, and Israel His reign.
The sea saw them and fled, the Jordan flowed backward.
Mountains skipped like rams, and hills like lambs.
What frightened you, sea, that you fled, Jordan that you flowed
backward, mountains that you skipped like rams, hills like lambs?
The earth trembles at the presence of the Lord, at the presence of
Jacob's God, who turns the rock into a pool of water, flint into a
fountain.

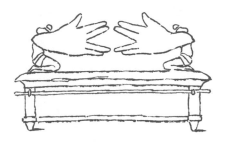

The matzot are covered, and we raise our cups of wine and say:

בָּרוּךְ אַתָּה יְיָ אֱלֹהֵינוּ מֶלֶךְ הָעוֹלָם אֲשֶׁר גְּאָלָנוּ וְגָאַל אֶת אֲבוֹתֵינוּ מִמִּצְרַיִם, וְהִגִּיעָנוּ לַלַּיְלָה הַזֶּה, לֶאֱכָל בּוֹ מַצָּה וּמָרוֹר. כֵּן יְיָ אֱלֹהֵינוּ וֵאלֹהֵי אֲבוֹתֵינוּ, הַגִּיעֵנוּ לְמוֹעֲדִים וְלִרְגָלִים אֲחֵרִים, הַבָּאִים לִקְרָאתֵנוּ לְשָׁלוֹם, שְׂמֵחִים בְּבִנְיַן עִירֶךָ, וְשָׂשִׂים בַּעֲבוֹדָתֶךָ. וְנֹאכַל שָׁם מִן הַזְּבָחִים וּמִן הַפְּסָחִים, אֲשֶׁר יַגִּיעַ דָּמָם עַל קִיר מִזְבַּחֲךָ לְרָצוֹן, וְנוֹדֶה לְךָ שִׁיר חָדָשׁ עַל גְּאֻלָּתֵנוּ וְעַל פְּדוּת נַפְשֵׁנוּ. בָּרוּךְ אַתָּה יְיָ גָּאַל יִשְׂרָאֵל.

Blessed are You, Lord our God, King of the Universe, who redeemed us and redeemed our ancestors from Egypt and brought us to this night to eat matzah and bitter herbs. May God, the God of our fathers, bring us to future holidays and festivals in peace, and allow us to see the rebuilding of Your city Jerusalem and share in the joy of Your service so that we may partake in Jerusalem of the ancient festive offerings. We shall then sing to You a new song, a song of redemption and salvation. Blessed are You, Lord our God, redeemer of Israel.

After reciting the blessing, we drink the second cup of wine while reclining.

בָּרוּךְ אַתָּה יְיָ אֱלֹהֵינוּ מֶלֶךְ הָעוֹלָם בּוֹרֵא פְּרִי הַגָּפֶן.

Blessed are You, Lord our God, King of the Universe, who creates the fruit of the vine.

Rachtzah

WASHING THE HANDS BEFORE
THE MEAL

We wash our hands in preparation for eating the matzah and say:

בָּרוּךְ אַתָּה יְיָ אֱלֹהֵינוּ מֶלֶךְ הָעוֹלָם אֲשֶׁר
קִדְּשָׁנוּ בְּמִצְוֹתָיו וְצִוָּנוּ עַל נְטִילַת יָדָיִם.

Blessed are You, Lord our God, King of the Universe, who
has sanctified us with His laws and commanded us to wash
our hands.

מוֹצִיא מַצָּה

Motzi Matzah

PRAYER FOR THE BEGINNING OF
THE MEAL AND BLESSING FOR
THE MATZAH

The head of the table lifts the three matzot and says:

בָּרוּךְ אַתָּה יְיָ אֱלֹהֵינוּ מֶלֶךְ הָעוֹלָם הַמּוֹצִיא
לֶחֶם מִן הָאָרֶץ.

**Blessed are You, Lord our God, King of the Universe, who
brings bread from the earth.**

*The head of the table puts the bottom matzah back in its place,
lifts the other two matzot and says:*

76

בָּרוּךְ אַתָּה יְיָ אֱלֹהֵינוּ מֶלֶךְ הָעוֹלָם אֲשֶׁר קִדְּשָׁנוּ בְּמִצְוֹתָיו וְצִוָּנוּ עַל אֲכִילַת מַצָּה.

Blessed are You, Lord our God, King of the Universe, who has sanctified us with His laws and commanded us to eat matzah.

The top and middle matzot are divided into pieces for each participant. All eat while reclining.

מָרוֹר

Maror

BLESSING FOR THE BITTER HERBS

We dip the bitter herbs in the charoset and say:

בָּרוּךְ אַתָּה יְיָ אֱלֹהֵינוּ מֶלֶךְ הָעוֹלָם אֲשֶׁר
קִדְּשָׁנוּ בְּמִצְוֹתָיו וְצִוָּנוּ עַל אֲכִילַת מָרוֹר.

Blessed are You, Lord our God, King of the Universe, who has sanctified us with His laws and commanded us to eat bitter herbs.

The bitter herbs are eaten without reclining.

כּוֹרֵךְ

Korech

HILLEL'S SANDWICH

The bottom matzah is broken so that each participant receives two pieces. All place bitter herbs between the two pieces of matzah and say:

זֵכֶר לְמִקְדָּשׁ כְּהִלֵּל. כֵּן עָשָׂה הִלֵּל בִּזְמַן שֶׁבֵּית הַמִּקְדָּשׁ הָיָה

קַיָּם: הָיָה כּוֹרֵךְ מַצָּה וּמָרוֹר וְאוֹכֵל בְּיַחַד, לְקַיֵּם מַה שֶׁנֶּאֱמַר:

עַל מַצּוֹת וּמְרֹרִים יֹאכְלֻהוּ.

In memory of the Temple: When the Temple still stood, Hillel would make a sandwich of matzah and maror and eat them together, for it is said, "They shall eat it with matzah and bitter herbs."

And for the rest of the Seder, the narrative will be but a song of praise to God. Present at the beginning of the story, God remains present to the end. The Seder, therefore, does not only tell the story of our suffering in exile, but also of our wait for redemption. And as we await redemption, the celebration of the word will yield to the celebration of the meal.

שֻׁלְחָן עוֹרֵךְ

Shulchan Orech

THE MEAL

The Seder plate containing the ritual symbols is removed from the table.

After the meal, the Seder plate is returned to the table.

צָפוּן

Tzafun

THE AFIKOMAN

At the conclusion of the meal, we eat the afikoman, as a reminder of the sacrificial lamb, which was eaten last. Since we no longer eat the Pesach sacrifice, for the Temple has been destroyed, it is the taste of the afikoman which must remain with us for the rest of the evening. But first we must buy it back from our children.

Long ago, it was the custom after leaving the table to go elsewhere for more festivities. Thus, sometimes the religious celebration degenerated into noisy revelry. To avoid this, it was decreed that after the afikoman, there would be no more eating. But there could be more drinking. And so, please fill your third cup.

The third cup of wine is filled.

בָּרֵךְ

Barech

SAYING GRACE

שִׁיר הַמַּעֲלוֹת: בְּשׁוּב יְיָ אֶת שִׁיבַת צִיּוֹן הָיִינוּ כְּחֹלְמִים. אָז

יִמָּלֵא שְׂחוֹק פִּינוּ, וּלְשׁוֹנֵנוּ רִנָּה; אָז יֹאמְרוּ בַגּוֹיִם, הִגְדִּיל יְיָ

לַעֲשׂוֹת עִם אֵלֶּה. הִגְדִּיל יְיָ לַעֲשׂוֹת עִמָּנוּ, הָיִינוּ שְׂמֵחִים.

שׁוּבָה יְיָ אֶת שְׁבִיתֵנוּ כַּאֲפִיקִים בַּנֶּגֶב. הַזֹּרְעִים בְּדִמְעָה, בְּרִנָּה

יִקְצֹרוּ. הָלוֹךְ יֵלֵךְ וּבָכֹה נֹשֵׂא מֶשֶׁךְ הַזָּרַע; בֹּא יָבֹא בְרִנָּה נֹשֵׂא

אֲלֻמֹּתָיו.

A song of ascents:

When the Lord returned the exiled to Zion we were like dreamers. Then our mouths filled with laughter and our tongues with joyous song. Then it was said among the nations, "The Lord has done great things for them." The Lord has done great things for us, we rejoiced. Lord, return our exiled like streams in the Negev. Those who sow with tears shall reap with joy. He who weeps while sowing will return rejoicing bearing sheaves.

בִּרְכַּת הַמָּזוֹן

When three or more men are present, the head of the table begins with the following introduction. If ten or more men are present, the words in parentheses are added.

The head of the table:

רַבּוֹתַי נְבָרֵךְ.

Let us say grace.

The other participants respond and the head of the table repeats:

יְהִי שֵׁם יְיָ מְבֹרָךְ מֵעַתָּה וְעַד עוֹלָם.

May the name of the Lord be blessed now and forever.

The head of the table:

בִּרְשׁוּת מָרָנָן וְרַבָּנָן וְרַבּוֹתַי נְבָרֵךְ (אֱלֹהֵינוּ) שֶׁאָכַלְנוּ מִשֶּׁלּוֹ.

With your permission, let us bless Him (our God)
whose food we have eaten.

The others respond and the head of the table repeats:

בָּרוּךְ (אֱלֹהֵינוּ) שֶׁאָכַלְנוּ מִשֶּׁלּוֹ וּבְטוּבוֹ חָיִינוּ.

Blessed be He (our God) whose food we have eaten and by
whose goodness we live.

All:

בָּרוּךְ הוּא וּבָרוּךְ שְׁמוֹ.

Blessed be He and blessed be His name.

בָּרוּךְ אַתָּה יְיָ אֱלֹהֵינוּ מֶלֶךְ הָעוֹלָם הַזָּן אֶת הָעוֹלָם כֻּלּוֹ בְּטוּבוֹ, בְּחֵן בְּחֶסֶד וּבְרַחֲמִים. הוּא נוֹתֵן לֶחֶם לְכָל בָּשָׂר, כִּי לְעוֹלָם חַסְדּוֹ. וּבְטוּבוֹ הַגָּדוֹל תָּמִיד לֹא חָסַר לָנוּ, וְאַל יֶחְסַר לָנוּ מָזוֹן לְעוֹלָם וָעֶד בַּעֲבוּר שְׁמוֹ הַגָּדוֹל. כִּי הוּא אֵל זָן וּמְפַרְנֵס לַכֹּל, וּמֵיטִיב לַכֹּל, וּמֵכִין מָזוֹן לְכָל בְּרִיּוֹתָיו אֲשֶׁר בָּרָא. בָּרוּךְ אַתָּה יְיָ הַזָּן אֶת הַכֹּל.

Blessed are You, Lord our God, King of the Universe, who sustains the entire world with goodness, grace, lovingkindness, and compassion. He gives bread to all, for His grace is everlasting. And in His great goodness we have never lacked anything and we will never be deprived of food for the sake of His great name. For He is God who provides for all and does good for all and prepares food for all His creatures whom He created. Blessed are You, Lord, who provides for all.

נוֹדֶה לְּךָ יְיָ אֱלֹהֵינוּ עַל שֶׁהִנְחַלְתָּ לַאֲבוֹתֵינוּ אֶרֶץ חֶמְדָּה טוֹבָה וּרְחָבָה, וְעַל שֶׁהוֹצֵאתָנוּ יְיָ אֱלֹהֵינוּ מֵאֶרֶץ מִצְרַיִם, וּפְדִיתָנוּ מִבֵּית עֲבָדִים, וְעַל בְּרִיתְךָ שֶׁחָתַמְתָּ בִּבְשָׂרֵנוּ, וְעַל תּוֹרָתְךָ שֶׁלִּמַּדְתָּנוּ, וְעַל חֻקֶּיךָ שֶׁהוֹדַעְתָּנוּ, וְעַל חַיִּים, חֵן וָחֶסֶד שֶׁחוֹנַנְתָּנוּ; וְעַל אֲכִילַת מָזוֹן, שָׁאַתָּה זָן וּמְפַרְנֵס אוֹתָנוּ תָּמִיד, בְּכָל יוֹם וּבְכָל עֵת וּבְכָל שָׁעָה.

We thank You, Lord our God, for the desirable, good, and spacious land which You gave our fathers as an inheritance and for liberating us from the land of Egypt and redeeming us from the house of bondage; and for Your covenant sealed in our flesh, for teaching us Your Torah, for making Your laws known to us, for life, grace, and kindness granted us; and for the food we eat and the sustenance You provide every day, every season, and every hour.

וְעַל הַכֹּל יְיָ אֱלֹהֵינוּ אֲנַחְנוּ מוֹדִים לָךְ, וּמְבָרְכִים אוֹתָךְ.

יִתְבָּרַךְ שִׁמְךָ בְּפִי כָל חַי תָּמִיד לְעוֹלָם וָעֶד, כַּכָּתוּב: וְאָכַלְתָּ

וְשָׂבָעְתָּ, וּבֵרַכְתָּ אֶת יְיָ אֱלֹהֶיךָ עַל הָאָרֶץ הַטֹּבָה אֲשֶׁר נָתַן

לָךְ. בָּרוּךְ אַתָּה יְיָ עַל הָאָרֶץ וְעַל הַמָּזוֹן.

And for all this, Lord our God, we thank and bless You. Blessed be Your name forever in the mouth of every living thing. As it is written: ''When you have eaten and are satisfied, you shall bless the Lord your God for the good land which He has given you.'' Blessed are You, Lord, for the land and for the food.

רַחֵם יְיָ אֱלֹהֵינוּ עַל יִשְׂרָאֵל עַמֶּךָ, וְעַל יְרוּשָׁלַיִם עִירֶךָ, וְעַל

צִיּוֹן מִשְׁכַּן כְּבוֹדֶךָ, וְעַל מַלְכוּת בֵּית דָּוִד מְשִׁיחֶךָ, וְעַל הַבַּיִת

הַגָּדוֹל וְהַקָּדוֹשׁ שֶׁנִּקְרָא שִׁמְךָ עָלָיו. אֱלֹהֵינוּ אָבִינוּ, רְעֵנוּ

זוּנֵנוּ, פַּרְנְסֵנוּ וְכַלְכְּלֵנוּ וְהַרְוִיחֵנוּ; וְהַרְוַח לָנוּ יְיָ אֱלֹהֵינוּ

מְהֵרָה מִכָּל צָרוֹתֵינוּ. וְנָא, אַל תַּצְרִיכֵנוּ יְיָ אֱלֹהֵינוּ לֹא לִידֵי

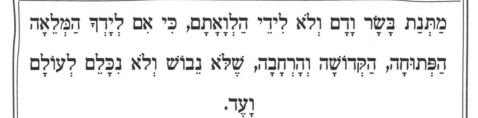

מַתְּנַת בָּשָׂר וָדָם וְלֹא לִידֵי הַלְוָאָתָם, כִּי אִם לְיָדְךָ הַמְּלֵאָה הַפְּתוּחָה, הַקְּדוֹשָׁה וְהָרְחָבָה, שֶׁלֹּא נֵבוֹשׁ וְלֹא נִכָּלֵם לְעוֹלָם וָעֶד.

Be merciful, Lord our God, on Israel Your people, on Jerusalem Your city, on Zion, the home of Your glory, on the royal House of David, Your anointed, and on the great and Holy Temple which is called by Your name. Our God, our Father, shepherd us, feed us, sustain us, maintain us, and relieve us soon from all our troubles. And may we never become dependent, Lord our God, on the gifts and loans of men, but may we rely solely on Your full, open, holy, and generous hand, so that we may never be ashamed or humiliated.

On the Sabbath the following paragraph is added:

(רְצֵה וְהַחֲלִיצֵנוּ יְיָ אֱלֹהֵינוּ בְּמִצְוֹתֶיךָ וּבְמִצְוַת יוֹם הַשְּׁבִיעִי, הַשַּׁבָּת הַגָּדוֹל וְהַקָּדוֹשׁ הַזֶּה, כִּי יוֹם זֶה גָּדוֹל וְקָדוֹשׁ הוּא לְפָנֶיךָ, לִשְׁבָּת בּוֹ וְלָנוּחַ בּוֹ בְּאַהֲבָה כְּמִצְוַת רְצוֹנֶךָ. וּבִרְצוֹנְךָ הָנַח לָנוּ יְיָ אֱלֹהֵינוּ שֶׁלֹּא תְהֵא צָרָה, וְיָגוֹן וַאֲנָחָה, בְּיוֹם

מְנוּחָתֵנוּ. וְהַרְאֵנוּ יְיָ אֱלֹהֵינוּ בְּנֶחָמַת צִיּוֹן עִירֶךָ, וּבְבִנְיַן

יְרוּשָׁלַיִם עִיר קָדְשֶׁךָ, כִּי אַתָּה הוּא בַּעַל הַיְשׁוּעוֹת וּבַעַל

הַנֶּחָמוֹת.)

[Favor and strengthen us, Lord our God, with Your commandments, and by the commandment of the seventh day, this great
and holy Sabbath. For this day is great and holy before You, that
we may cease and rest on it, with love, according to Your will.
And may it be Your will, Lord our God, that there be no trouble,
sorrow, or anguish on our day of rest. And may we witness, Lord
our God, the consolation of Zion, Your city, and the rebuilding of
Your holy city Jerusalem. For You are the Master of redemption
and consolation.]

אֱלֹהֵינוּ וֵאלֹהֵי אֲבוֹתֵינוּ, יַעֲלֶה וְיָבֹא, וְיַגִּיעַ וְיֵרָאֶה, וְיֵרָצֶה

וְיִשָּׁמַע, וְיִפָּקֵד וְיִזָּכֵר זִכְרוֹנֵנוּ וּפִקְדוֹנֵנוּ, וְזִכְרוֹן אֲבוֹתֵינוּ,

וְזִכְרוֹן מָשִׁיחַ בֶּן דָּוִד עַבְדֶּךָ, וְזִכְרוֹן יְרוּשָׁלַיִם עִיר קָדְשֶׁךָ,

וְזִכְרוֹן כָּל עַמְּךָ בֵּית יִשְׂרָאֵל לְפָנֶיךָ, לִפְלֵיטָה וּלְטוֹבָה, לְחֵן

וּלְחֶסֶד וּלְרַחֲמִים, לְחַיִּים וּלְשָׁלוֹם, בְּיוֹם חַג הַמַּצּוֹת הַזֶּה.

זָכְרֵנוּ יְיָ אֱלֹהֵינוּ בּוֹ לְטוֹבָה, וּפָקְדֵנוּ בוֹ לִבְרָכָה, וְהוֹשִׁיעֵנוּ

בוֹ לְחַיִּים. וּבִדְבַר יְשׁוּעָה וְרַחֲמִים חוּס וְחָנֵּנוּ, וְרַחֵם עָלֵינוּ

וְהוֹשִׁיעֵנוּ כִּי אֵלֶיךָ עֵינֵינוּ, כִּי אֵל מֶלֶךְ חַנּוּן וְרַחוּם אָתָּה.

87

Our God and God of our fathers, may there ascend, come, reach, be seen, be favored, be heard, be counted and remembered before You the memory and recollection of ourselves, the memory of our fathers, the memory of the Messiah son of David Your servant, the memory of Jerusalem Your holy city, and the memory of all Your people, the House of Israel, for deliverance, for goodness, for grace, for kindness, for compassion, for life, and for peace, on this the festival of matzah. Remember us on this day, Lord our God, for good, consider us for a blessing and save us for life. Through the promise of redemption and mercy, have pity on us, pardon us, have compassion for us, and save us, for our eyes are turned to You, for You are a gracious and merciful God and King.

וּבְנֵה יְרוּשָׁלַיִם עִיר הַקֹּדֶשׁ בִּמְהֵרָה בְיָמֵינוּ. בָּרוּךְ אַתָּה יְיָ
בּוֹנֵה בְרַחֲמָיו יְרוּשָׁלָיִם. אָמֵן.

Rebuild Jerusalem, the holy city, speedily in our own days. Blessed are You, Lord, who in His mercy rebuilds Jerusalem. Amen.

בָּרוּךְ אַתָּה יְיָ אֱלֹהֵינוּ מֶלֶךְ הָעוֹלָם, הָאֵל, אָבִינוּ, מַלְכֵּנוּ,
אַדִירֵנוּ, בּוֹרְאֵנוּ, גּוֹאֲלֵנוּ, יוֹצְרֵנוּ, קְדוֹשֵׁנוּ, קְדוֹשׁ יַעֲקֹב,
רוֹעֵנוּ, רוֹעֵה יִשְׂרָאֵל, הַמֶּלֶךְ הַטּוֹב וְהַמֵּיטִיב לַכֹּל, שֶׁבְּכָל יוֹם
וָיוֹם הוּא הֵיטִיב, הוּא מֵטִיב, הוּא יֵיטִיב לָנוּ. הוּא גְמָלָנוּ, הוּא
גוֹמְלֵנוּ, הוּא יִגְמְלֵנוּ לָעַד, לְחֵן וּלְחֶסֶד וּלְרַחֲמִים וּלְרֶוַח,

הַצָּלָה וְהַצְלָחָה, בְּרָכָה וִישׁוּעָה, נֶחָמָה פַּרְנָסָה וְכַלְכָּלָה, וְרַחֲמִים וְחַיִּים וְשָׁלוֹם וְכָל טוֹב, וּמִכָּל טוּב לְעוֹלָם אַל יְחַסְּרֵנוּ.

Blessed are You, Lord our God, King of the Universe, our Father, our King, our Mighty One, our Creator, our Redeemer, our Maker, our Holy One, the Holy One of Jacob, our Shepherd, the Shepherd of Israel; the good King who is good to all and will always do good for us. May You continue to grant us Your grace, kindness, mercy, and deliverance, success, blessing, and redemption and comfort, support, sustenance, compassion, life and peace and all that is good. And may You never allow us to be deprived of anything that is good.

הָרַחֲמָן, הוּא יִמְלֹךְ עָלֵינוּ לְעוֹלָם וָעֶד.

הָרַחֲמָן, הוּא יִתְבָּרֵךְ בַּשָּׁמַיִם וּבָאָרֶץ.

הָרַחֲמָן, הוּא יִשְׁתַּבַּח לְדוֹר דּוֹרִים, וְיִתְפָּאַר בָּנוּ לָעַד וּלְנֵצַח נְצָחִים, וְיִתְהַדַּר בָּנוּ לָעַד וּלְעוֹלְמֵי עוֹלָמִים.

הָרַחֲמָן, הוּא יְפַרְנְסֵנוּ בְּכָבוֹד.

הָרַחֲמָן, הוּא יִשְׁבֹּר עֻלֵּנוּ מֵעַל צַוָּארֵנוּ וְהוּא יוֹלִיכֵנוּ קוֹמְמִיּוּת לְאַרְצֵנוּ.

הָרַחֲמָן, הוּא יִשְׁלַח בְּרָכָה מְרֻבָּה בַּבַּיִת הַזֶּה, וְעַל שֻׁלְחָן זֶה שֶׁאָכַלְנוּ עָלָיו.

הָרַחֲמָן, הוּא יִשְׁלַח לָנוּ אֶת אֵלִיָּהוּ הַנָּבִיא, זָכוּר לַטּוֹב, וִיבַשֶּׂר לָנוּ בְּשׂוֹרוֹת טוֹבוֹת, יְשׁוּעוֹת וְנֶחָמוֹת.

הָרַחֲמָן, הוּא יְבָרֵךְ, אֶת (אָבִי מוֹרִי) בַּעַל הַבַּיִת הַזֶּה וְאֶת (אִמִּי מוֹרָתִי) בַּעֲלַת הַבַּיִת הַזֶּה, אוֹתָם וְאֶת בֵּיתָם וְאֶת זַרְעָם וְאֶת כָּל אֲשֶׁר לָהֶם, אוֹתָנוּ וְאֶת כָּל אֲשֶׁר לָנוּ, (וְאֶת כָּל הַמְסֻבִּים כַּאן) כְּמוֹ שֶׁנִּתְבָּרְכוּ אֲבוֹתֵינוּ אַבְרָהָם יִצְחָק וְיַעֲקֹב בַּכֹּל מִכֹּל כֹּל, כֵּן יְבָרֵךְ אוֹתָנוּ, כֻּלָּנוּ יַחַד, בִּבְרָכָה שְׁלֵמָה, וְנֹאמַר אָמֵן.

בַּמָּרוֹם יְלַמְּדוּ עֲלֵיהֶם וְעָלֵינוּ זְכוּת, שֶׁתְּהֵא לְמִשְׁמֶרֶת שָׁלוֹם. וְנִשָּׂא בְרָכָה מֵאֵת יְיָ, וּצְדָקָה מֵאֱלֹהֵי יִשְׁעֵנוּ, וְנִמְצָא חֵן וְשֵׂכֶל טוֹב בְּעֵינֵי אֱלֹהִים וְאָדָם.

May the Merciful reign over us forever.
May the Merciful be blessed in heaven and on earth.
May the Merciful be blessed in every generation, may He be glorified through us for eternity and eternity, and may He be honored through us forever and ever.
May the Merciful provide for us honorably.
May the Merciful break the oppressor's yoke and lead us with dignity to our land.
May the Merciful send numerous blessings on this house and on this table at which we have eaten.
May the Merciful send us the prophet Elijah, remembered for his goodness, who will bring us good tidings of salvation and consolation.

May the Merciful bless (my father and teacher), the master of this house, and my (mother and teacher), the lady of this house, they and their home, their children, and all that is theirs. Bless us and all that is ours (and may He bless all who are gathered here) as our fathers Abraham, Isaac, and Jacob were blessed in all things; so may He bless all of us together with a full blessing and let us say: Amen.

In heaven, invoke our merits to assure peace. May we receive a blessing from the Lord and charity from the God of our deliverance, and may we find grace and good understanding in the sight of God and man.

On the Sabbath add the following bracketed sentence:

(הָרַחֲמָן, הוּא יַנְחִילֵנוּ יוֹם שֶׁכֻּלּוֹ שַׁבָּת וּמְנוּחָה לְחַיֵּי הָעוֹלָמִים.)

הָרַחֲמָן, הוּא יַנְחִילֵנוּ יוֹם שֶׁכֻּלּוֹ טוֹב.

[May the Merciful grant us a day solely of Sabbath and rest in the world to come.]

May the Merciful grant us a day that is solely good.

הָרַחֲמָן, הוּא יְזַכֵּנוּ לִימוֹת הַמָּשִׁיחַ וּלְחַיֵּי הָעוֹלָם הַבָּא. מִגְדּוֹל יְשׁוּעוֹת מַלְכּוֹ וְעֹשֶׂה חֶסֶד לִמְשִׁיחוֹ, לְדָוִד וּלְזַרְעוֹ עַד עוֹלָם. עֹשֶׂה שָׁלוֹם בִּמְרוֹמָיו, הוּא יַעֲשֶׂה שָׁלוֹם עָלֵינוּ וְעַל כָּל יִשְׂרָאֵל, וְאִמְרוּ אָמֵן.

May the Merciful find us worthy to witness the days of the Messiah and the life of the world to come. "He is a tower of victory to His king, and shows grace to His anointed, David and his descendants forever." May He who makes peace in heaven grant peace to us and to all Israel and let us say: Amen.

יְראוּ אֶת יְיָ קְדֹשָׁיו, כִּי אֵין מַחְסוֹר לִירֵאָיו. כְּפִירִים רָשׁוּ וְרָעֵבוּ, וְדֹרְשֵׁי יְיָ לֹא יַחְסְרוּ כָל טוֹב. הוֹדוּ לַיְיָ כִּי טוֹב, כִּי לְעוֹלָם חַסְדּוֹ. פּוֹתֵחַ אֶת יָדֶךָ, וּמַשְׂבִּיעַ לְכָל חַי רָצוֹן. בָּרוּךְ הַגֶּבֶר אֲשֶׁר יִבְטַח בַּיְיָ, וְהָיָה יְיָ מִבְטַחוֹ. נַעַר הָיִיתִי גַּם זָקַנְתִּי, וְלֹא רָאִיתִי צַדִּיק נֶעֱזָב, וְזַרְעוֹ מְבַקֶּשׁ־לָחֶם. יְיָ עֹז לְעַמּוֹ יִתֵּן, יְיָ יְבָרֵךְ אֶת עַמּוֹ בַשָּׁלוֹם.

Revere the Lord, you His holy ones; for those who revere Him nothing is lacking. Young lions suffer and are hungry, but those who seek God shall not be deprived of any good thing. Give thanks to the Lord for He is good. For His grace is everlasting. You open Your hand and satisfy all life. Blessed is the man who trusts in God, the Lord will be his protection. I was young and now I am old, yet I have never witnessed a righteous man abandoned and his children begging for bread. The Lord will give strength to His people; the Lord will bless His people with peace.

בָּרוּךְ אַתָּה יְיָ אֱלֹהֵינוּ מֶלֶךְ הָעוֹלָם בּוֹרֵא פְּרִי הַגָּפֶן.

Blessed are You, Lord our God, King of the Universe, who creates the fruit of the vine.

Pour the fourth cup of wine, and a fifth cup for the prophet Elijah.

Please do not forget the prophet Elijah's cup. Tradition holds that the greatest miracle-maker among the prophets visits all Jewish homes to drink wine from his own cup. There is a discussion in the Talmud: How many cups is one supposed to drink during the Seder? Some sages said four, explaining that God used four words when he promised to free Israel. These words were: *Vegaalti* (and I shall redeem you), *Velaka'hti* (and I shall take you), *Vehotzeti* (and I shall remove you), *Vehitzalti* (and I shall save you). But other sages said that God used a fifth word, *Veheveti* (and I shall bring you). For lack of consensus, they decided to drink four cups, but to fill five. The fifth was intended for the prophet Elijah, who more than any other prophet is linked to the ultimate redemption of Israel.

Elijah is friend and companion to all who need friendship and comfort. He is the mysterious stranger who arrives at precisely the right moment, to bring hope to those in despair.

We have no better defender in heaven than Elijah. Not only is

he forever concerned with Jewish suffering, but he also shares his concern with God. He is the chronicler, the historian, of Jewish distress. He records every tragic event, every upheaval, every tear; thanks to him nothing is lost. His most glorious role is that of witness. He is the memory of the Jewish people.

Elijah, the miracle-maker, the prophet of consolation, is also the peacemaker. We think of him as the bearer of secrets, including the ultimate secret. One day he will come to stay, and on that day, he will accompany the Messiah, with whose destiny he is linked. Elijah will resolve all questions, resolve all tensions. And on that day also, it is Elijah who will tell us how many cups we are supposed to drink during the Seder.

The door is opened.

In certain communities it was customary for all to stand as the door was opened to welcome the prophet Elijah.

שְׁפֹךְ חֲמָתְךָ אֶל הַגּוֹיִם אֲשֶׁר לֹא יְדָעוּךָ, וְעַל מַמְלָכוֹת אֲשֶׁר בְּשִׁמְךָ לֹא קָרָאוּ. כִּי אָכַל אֶת יַעֲקֹב, וְאֶת נָוֵהוּ הֵשַׁמּוּ. שְׁפָךְ עֲלֵיהֶם זַעְמֶךָ, וַחֲרוֹן אַפְּךָ יַשִּׂיגֵם. תִּרְדֹּף בְּאַף וְתַשְׁמִידֵם מִתַּחַת שְׁמֵי יְיָ.

Pour Your anger and Your wrath on the heathen nations that do not know You and the sinful kingdoms that do not call Your name. For they have devoured Jacob and destroyed his dwelling place. Pour Your fury on them, and let Your anger reach them. Pursue them in indignation, and annihilate them from under the firmament of God.

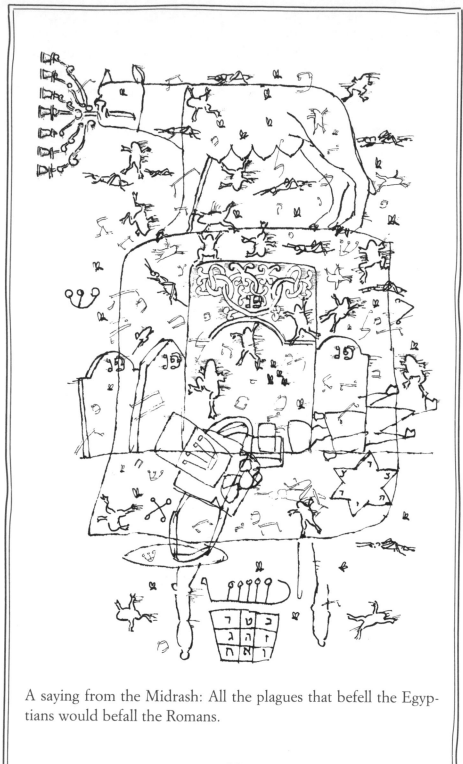

A saying from the Midrash: All the plagues that befell the Egyptians would befall the Romans.

A solemn prayer, it calls for harsh punishment of the enemies. Why such vindictive words? Why do we say them in the presence of the prophet of consolation, and why do we do this with the door open? To show the world that we have nothing to hide? To let the wicked know that we mean them? Perhaps.

In honor of the prophet, we sing a song bearing his name:

אֵלִיָּהוּ הַנָּבִיא, אֵלִיָּהוּ הַתִּשְׁבִּי,

אֵלִיָּהוּ אֵלִיָּהוּ, אֵלִיָּהוּ הַגִּלְעָדִי,

בִּמְהֵרָה בְיָמֵינוּ יָבֹא אֵלֵינוּ

עִם מָשִׁיחַ בֶּן דָּוִד.

Eliyahu (Elijah) the prophet, Eliyahu the Tishbite from Gilead. He will soon be in our midst, accompanying the Messiah, son of David.

The door is closed.

Ani Maamin

אֲנִי מַאֲמִין בֶּאֱמוּנָה שְׁלֵמָה בְּבִיאַת הַמָּשִׁיחַ. וְאַף עַל פִּי

שֶׁיִּתְמַהְמֵהַּ, עִם כָּל־זֶה אֲחַכֶּה לוֹ בְּכָל־יוֹם שֶׁיָּבֹא.

I believe with all my heart in the coming of the Messiah and although he will be late, I will wait each and every day for his arrival.

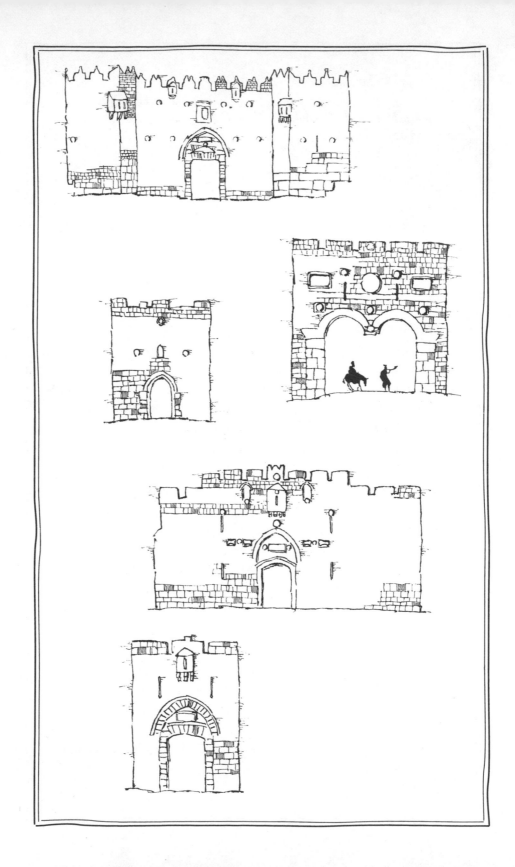

The following text is excerpted from "Ani Maamin," a poem by Elie Wiesel set to music by Darius Milhaud, which had its premiere at Carnegie Hall on November 13, 1973.

A camp.
An inmate.
A creature without a name,
A man without a face,
Without a destiny.
It is night,
The first night of Passover.
The camp is asleep,
He alone is awake.
He talks to himself
Soundlessly.
I hear his words,
I capture his silence.
To himself, to me,
He is saying:
I have not partaken of
    matzot,
Nor of maror.

I have not emptied the four cups,
Symbols of the four deliverances.
I did not invite
The hungry
To share my repast—
Or even my hunger.
No longer have I a son
To ask me
The four questions—
No longer have I the strength
To answer. . . .
The parable of Had Gadya is mis-
    leading:
God will not come
To slay the slaughterer.
The innocent victims
Will go unavenged.
The ancient wish—
Leshana habaa bi-Yerushalaim—

Will not be granted.
I shall not be in Jerusalem
Next year.
Or anywhere else.
Next year
I shall not be.
And then,
How do I know
That Jerusalem is there,
Far away,
That Jerusalem is not here?
Still, I recite the Haggadah
As though I believe in it.
And I await the prophet
    Elijah,
As I did long ago.

I open my heart to him
And say:
Welcome, prophet of the promise,
Welcome, herald of redemption.
Come, share in my story,
Come, rejoice with the dead
That we are.
Empty the cup
That bears your name.
Come to us,
Come to us on this Passover night:
We are in Egypt
And we are the ones
To suffer God's plagues.
Come, friend of the poor,
Defender of the oppressed,
Come.
I shall wait for you.
And even if you disappoint me
I shall go on waiting,
Ani Maamin.

הַלֵּל

Hallel

PSALMS OF PRAISE

לָנוּ, יְיָ, לֹא לָנוּ, כִּי לְשִׁמְךָ תֵּן כָּבוֹד, עַל **לֹא**

חַסְדְּךָ, עַל אֲמִתֶּךָ. לָמָּה יֹאמְרוּ הַגּוֹיִם, אַיֵּה

נָא אֱלֹהֵיהֶם. וֵאלֹהֵינוּ בַשָּׁמָיִם; כֹּל אֲשֶׁר חָפֵץ עָשָׂה. עֲצַבֵּיהֶם

כֶּסֶף וְזָהָב, מַעֲשֵׂה יְדֵי אָדָם. פֶּה לָהֶם וְלֹא יְדַבֵּרוּ, עֵינַיִם לָהֶם

וְלֹא יִרְאוּ. אָזְנַיִם לָהֶם וְלֹא יִשְׁמָעוּ, אַף לָהֶם וְלֹא יְרִיחוּן.

יְדֵיהֶם וְלֹא יְמִישׁוּן, רַגְלֵיהֶם וְלֹא יְהַלֵּכוּ; לֹא יֶהְגּוּ בִּגְרוֹנָם.

כְּמוֹהֶם יִהְיוּ עֹשֵׂיהֶם, כֹּל אֲשֶׁר בֹּטֵחַ בָּהֶם. יִשְׂרָאֵל, בְּטַח בַּייָ

עֶזְרָם וּמָגִנָּם הוּא. בֵּית אַהֲרֹן, בִּטְחוּ בַייָ עֶזְרָם וּמָגִנָּם הוּא.

יִרְאֵי יְיָ, בִּטְחוּ בַייָ עֶזְרָם וּמָגִנָּם הוּא.

יְיָ זְכָרָנוּ יְבָרֵךְ, יְבָרֵךְ אֶת בֵּית יִשְׂרָאֵל, יְבָרֵךְ אֶת בֵּית אַהֲרֹן.

יְבָרֵךְ יִרְאֵי יְיָ, הַקְּטַנִּים עִם הַגְּדֹלִים. יֹסֵף יְיָ עֲלֵיכֶם, עֲלֵיכֶם

וְעַל בְּנֵיכֶם. בְּרוּכִים אַתֶּם לַייָ, עֹשֵׂה שָׁמַיִם וָאָרֶץ. הַשָּׁמַיִם

שָׁמַיִם לַייָ, וְהָאָרֶץ נָתַן לִבְנֵי אָדָם. לֹא הַמֵּתִים יְהַלְלוּ יָהּ,

וְלֹא כָּל יֹרְדֵי דוּמָה. וַאֲנַחְנוּ נְבָרֵךְ יָהּ מֵעַתָּה וְעַד עוֹלָם;

הַלְלוּיָהּ.

Psalm 115

Not for us alone, God, not for us alone, but to Your name give
   glory, for the sake of Your grace and Your truth.
Why should the nations say: "Where is their God?"
Our God is in the heavens, and He accomplishes all that He wills.
Their idols are silver and gold, the work of human hands.
They have mouths but cannot speak, eyes but cannot see.
They have ears but cannot hear, noses but cannot smell.
They have hands but cannot feel, feet but cannot walk.
They cannot utter a sound in their throats.
Their makers, and all who trust in them, shall become like them.
Israel, trust in the Lord!
He is their help and shield.
House of Aaron, trust in the Lord!

He is their help and shield.

Let those who revere the Lord, trust in the Lord!

He is their help and shield.

The Lord remembers us. He will bless us; He will bless the House of Israel.

He will bless the House of Aaron.

He will bless those who revere God, young and old.

May God add to your blessings, yours and your children's.

May you be blessed by the Lord, who created heaven and earth.

The heavens belong to the Lord, but the earth He gave to mankind.

The dead cannot praise the Lord, nor those who sink into muteness.

But we shall praise the Lord now and always. Halleluyah!

אָהַבְתִּי כִּי יִשְׁמַע יְיָ אֶת קוֹלִי, תַּחֲנוּנָי. כִּי הִטָּה אָזְנוֹ לִי,

וּבְיָמַי אֶקְרָא. אֲפָפוּנִי חֶבְלֵי מָוֶת, וּמְצָרֵי שְׁאוֹל מְצָאוּנִי; צָרָה

וְיָגוֹן אֶמְצָא. וּבְשֵׁם יְיָ אֶקְרָא, אָנָּה יְיָ, מַלְּטָה נַפְשִׁי. חַנּוּן יְיָ

וְצַדִּיק, וֵאלֹהֵינוּ מְרַחֵם. שֹׁמֵר פְּתָאִים יְיָ; דַּלּוֹתִי וְלִי יְהוֹשִׁיעַ.

שׁוּבִי נַפְשִׁי לִמְנוּחָיְכִי, כִּי יְיָ גָּמַל עָלָיְכִי. כִּי חִלַּצְתָּ נַפְשִׁי מִמָּוֶת, אֶת עֵינִי מִן דִּמְעָה, אֶת רַגְלִי מִדֶּחִי. אֶתְהַלֵּךְ לִפְנֵי יְיָ, בְּאַרְצוֹת הַחַיִּים. הֶאֱמַנְתִּי כִּי אֲדַבֵּר, אֲנִי עָנִיתִי מְאֹד. אֲנִי אָמַרְתִּי בְחָפְזִי, כָּל הָאָדָם כֹּזֵב.

מָה אָשִׁיב לַיְיָ כָּל תַּגְמוּלוֹהִי עָלָי. כּוֹס יְשׁוּעוֹת אֶשָּׂא, וּבְשֵׁם יְיָ אֶקְרָא. נְדָרַי לַיְיָ אֲשַׁלֵּם, נֶגְדָה־נָּא לְכָל עַמּוֹ. יָקָר בְּעֵינֵי יְיָ הַמָּוְתָה לַחֲסִידָיו אָנָּה יְיָ, כִּי אֲנִי עַבְדֶּךָ, אֲנִי עַבְדְּךָ בֶּן אֲמָתֶךָ; פִּתַּחְתָּ לְמוֹסֵרָי. לְךָ אֶזְבַּח זֶבַח תּוֹדָה, וּבְשֵׁם יְיָ אֶקְרָא. נְדָרַי לַיְיָ אֲשַׁלֵּם, נֶגְדָה־נָּא לְכָל עַמּוֹ. בְּחַצְרוֹת בֵּית יְיָ, בְּתוֹכֵכִי יְרוּשָׁלַיִם; הַלְלוּיָהּ.

Psalm 116

I love God for hearing my voice, and receiving my pleas; because
   He turns His ear to me when I call.
I am surrounded by the bonds of death, and caught in the straits
   of the abyss; I encountered trouble and sorrow.
And I called on the name of the Lord: "I beseech You, God, save
   my soul."
The Lord is gracious and righteous, our God is compassionate.
The Lord protects the simple; I was humbled and He saved me.
Be at peace again, my soul, for the Lord has been kind to you.

The Lord has delivered me from death, my eyes from tears, and
my feet from stumbling. I shall walk before the Lord in the land
of the living.
I kept my faith even when I cried out hastily in my affliction, "All
men are liars."
How can I repay the Lord for all His blessings?
I raise the cup of deliverance and invoke the Lord's name.
I will redeem my vows to the Lord in the presence of all His
people.
The death of His faithful is painful in the Lord's sight.
Lord, I am Your servant, the child of your maidservant; You have
untied the ropes that bound me.
I will bring to You an offering of thanksgiving and will invoke the
name of the Lord.
I will redeem my vows to the Lord in the presence of all His
people, in the courts of the House of the Lord, inside Jerusalem.
Halleluyah!

הַלְלוּ אֶת יְיָ, כָּל גּוֹיִם, שַׁבְּחֽוּהוּ, כָּל הָאֻמִּים. כִּי גָבַר עָלֵֽינוּ

חַסְדּוֹ, וֶאֱמֶת יְיָ לְעוֹלָם; הַלְלוּיָהּ.

Psalm 117

Praise the Lord, all nations.
Exalt Him, all peoples. Great is His kindness toward us; His
faithfulness is everlasting.
Halleluyah!

הוֹדוּ לַיָי כִּי טוֹב   כִּי לְעוֹלָם חַסְדּוֹ.

יֹאמַר נָא יִשְׂרָאֵל   כִּי לְעוֹלָם חַסְדּוֹ.

יֹאמְרוּ נָא בֵית אַהֲרֹן   כִּי לְעוֹלָם חַסְדּוֹ.

יֹאמְרוּ נָא יִרְאֵי יָי   כִּי לְעוֹלָם חַסְדּוֹ.

מִן הַמֵּצַר קָרָאתִי יָּה, עָנָנִי בַמֶּרְחָב יָה. יְיָ לִי, לֹא אִירָא; מַה יַּעֲשֶׂה לִי אָדָם. יְיָ לִי בְּעֹזְרָי, וַאֲנִי אֶרְאֶה בְשֹׂנְאָי. טוֹב לַחֲסוֹת בַּיְיָ מִבְּטֹחַ בָּאָדָם. טוֹב לַחֲסוֹת בַּיְיָ מִבְּטֹחַ בִּנְדִיבִים. כָּל גּוֹיִם סְבָבוּנִי בְּשֵׁם יְיָ, כִּי אֲמִילַם. סַבּוּנִי גַם סְבָבוּנִי בְּשֵׁם יְיָ, כִּי אֲמִילַם. סַבּוּנִי כִדְבוֹרִים, דֹּעֲכוּ כְּאֵשׁ קוֹצִים; בְּשֵׁם יְיָ, כִּי אֲמִילַם. דָּחֹה דְחִיתַנִי לִנְפֹּל, וַיְיָ עֲזָרָנִי. עָזִּי וְזִמְרָת יָּה, וַיְהִי לִי לִישׁוּעָה. קוֹל רִנָּה וִישׁוּעָה בְּאָהֳלֵי צַדִּיקִים; יְמִין יְיָ עֹשָׂה חָיִל. יְמִין יְיָ רוֹמֵמָה, יְמִין יְיָ עֹשָׂה חָיִל. לֹא אָמוּת כִּי אֶחְיֶה, וַאֲסַפֵּר מַעֲשֵׂי יָּה, יַסֹּר יִסְּרַנִּי יָּה, וְלַמָּוֶת לֹא נְתָנָנִי. פִּתְחוּ לִי שַׁעֲרֵי צֶדֶק; אָבֹא בָם, אוֹדֶה יָּה. זֶה הַשַּׁעַר לַיְיָ, צַדִּיקִים יָבֹאוּ בוֹ.

אוֹדְךָ כִּי עֲנִיתָנִי, וַתְּהִי לִי לִישׁוּעָה.

אֶבֶן מָאֲסוּ הַבּוֹנִים, הָיְתָה לְרֹאשׁ פִּנָּה.

מֵאֵת יְיָ הָיְתָה זֹּאת, הִיא נִפְלָאת בְּעֵינֵינוּ.

זֶה הַיּוֹם עָשָׂה יְיָ, נָגִילָה וְנִשְׂמְחָה בוֹ.

אָנָּא יְיָ הוֹשִׁיעָה נָא. אָנָּא יְיָ הוֹשִׁיעָה נָא.

אָנָּא יְיָ הַצְלִיחָה נָא. אָנָּא יְיָ הַצְלִיחָה נָא.

Each of the following four verses is repeated.

בָּרוּךְ הַבָּא בְּשֵׁם יְיָ, בֵּרַכְנוּכֶם מִבֵּית יְיָ.

אֵל יְיָ וַיָּאֶר לָנוּ, אִסְרוּ חַג בַּעֲבֹתִים, עַד קַרְנוֹת הַמִּזְבֵּחַ.

אֵלִי אַתָּה וְאוֹדֶךָּ אֱלֹהַי אֲרוֹמְמֶךָּ.

הוֹדוּ לַיְיָ כִּי טוֹב, כִּי לְעוֹלָם חַסְדּוֹ.

Psalm 118

Praise the Lord, for He is good; for His grace is everlasting.
Let Israel declare: For His grace is everlasting.
Let the House of Aaron declare: For His grace is everlasting.
Let those who revere the Lord declare: For His grace is everlasting.
In my distress I called to the Lord; He answered by setting me free.
The Lord is with me, I have no fear; what can man do to me?
The Lord is with me as my helper; I will witness the defeat of my
    enemies.

It is better to rely on the Lord than to trust in humankind.

It is better to rely on the Lord than to trust in princes.

Although many nations surrounded me, in the Lord's name I overcame them.

They swarmed around me like bees, they were extinguished like fiery thorns. In the Lord's name I overcame them.

They pushed me hard to make me fall, but the Lord helped me.

The Lord is my strength and my might and my deliverance.

The joyous song of deliverance is heard in the dwellings of the righteous:

> "The right hand of the Lord is triumphant!
>
> The right hand of the Lord is exalted!
>
> The right hand of the Lord is triumphant!"

I shall not die but live to tell the works of the Lord.

The Lord severely punished me but He did not let me die.

Open the gates of the righteous for me that I may enter and praise the Lord.

This is the gate of the Lord that the righteous shall enter.

Each of the following verses is repeated.

I thank You for having answered me; You have become my salvation.

A stone rejected by the builders has become the cornerstone.

This is the Lord's doing; it is marvelous in our sight.

This is the day the Lord has made; let us rejoice and be happy.

We implore You, Lord, deliver us!

We implore You, Lord, let us prosper!

Blessed are those who come in the name of the Lord.

We bless You from the House of the Lord.

The Lord is God; He has given us light.

Bind the festive offering to the corners of the altar.

You are my God and I will praise You.

You are my God and I will exalt You.

Praise the Lord for He is good; for His grace is everlasting.

יְהַלְלוּךָ יְיָ אֱלֹהֵינוּ, כָּל מַעֲשֶׂיךָ; וַחֲסִידֶיךָ, צַדִּיקִים עוֹשֵׂי רְצוֹנֶךָ, וְכָל עַמְּךָ בֵּית יִשְׂרָאֵל, בְּרִנָּה יוֹדוּ וִיבָרְכוּ, וִישַׁבְּחוּ וִיפָאֲרוּ, וִירוֹמְמוּ וְיַעֲרִיצוּ, וְיַקְדִּישׁוּ וְיַמְלִיכוּ אֶת שִׁמְךָ מַלְכֵּנוּ. כִּי לְךָ טוֹב לְהוֹדוֹת, וּלְשִׁמְךָ נָאֶה לְזַמֵּר, כִּי מֵעוֹלָם וְעַד עוֹלָם אַתָּה אֵל.

May all life praise You, Lord our God. And Your pious, the righteous who do Your will, and all Your people, the House of Israel shall thank You in joyous song. They shall bless, revere, praise, exalt, admire, and sanctify Your sovereign name, our King. For it is good to thank You and it is fitting to sing praises to Your name. You are God from eternity to eternity.

הוֹדוּ

לַיְיָ כִּי טוֹב   כִּי לְעוֹלָם חַסְדּוֹ.

הוֹדוּ לֵאלֹהֵי הָאֱלֹהִים   כִּי לְעוֹלָם חַסְדּוֹ.

הוֹדוּ לַאֲדֹנֵי הָאֲדֹנִים   כִּי לְעוֹלָם חַסְדּוֹ.

לְעֹשֵׂה נִפְלָאוֹת גְּדֹלוֹת לְבַדּוֹ   כִּי לְעוֹלָם חַסְדּוֹ.

לְעֹשֵׂה הַשָּׁמַיִם בִּתְבוּנָה   כִּי לְעוֹלָם חַסְדּוֹ.

לְרוֹקַע הָאָרֶץ עַל הַמָּיִם   כִּי לְעוֹלָם חַסְדּוֹ.

כִּי לְעוֹלָם חַסְדּוֹ.	לְעֹשֵׂה אוֹרִים גְּדֹלִים
כִּי לְעוֹלָם חַסְדּוֹ.	אֶת הַשֶּׁמֶשׁ לְמֶמְשֶׁלֶת בַּיּוֹם
כִּי לְעוֹלָם חַסְדּוֹ.	אֶת הַיָּרֵחַ וְכוֹכָבִים לְמֶמְשְׁלוֹת בַּלָּיְלָה
כִּי לְעוֹלָם חַסְדּוֹ.	לְמַכֵּה מִצְרַיִם בִּבְכוֹרֵיהֶם
כִּי לְעוֹלָם חַסְדּוֹ.	וַיּוֹצֵא יִשְׂרָאֵל מִתּוֹכָם
כִּי לְעוֹלָם חַסְדּוֹ.	בְּיָד חֲזָקָה וּבִזְרוֹעַ נְטוּיָה
כִּי לְעוֹלָם חַסְדּוֹ.	לְגֹזֵר יַם סוּף לִגְזָרִים
כִּי לְעוֹלָם חַסְדּוֹ.	וְהֶעֱבִיר יִשְׂרָאֵל בְּתוֹכוֹ
כִּי לְעוֹלָם חַסְדּוֹ.	וְנִעֵר פַּרְעֹה וְחֵילוֹ בְיַם סוּף
כִּי לְעוֹלָם חַסְדּוֹ.	לְמוֹלִיךְ עַמּוֹ בַּמִּדְבָּר
כִּי לְעוֹלָם חַסְדּוֹ.	לְמַכֵּה מְלָכִים גְּדֹלִים
כִּי לְעוֹלָם חַסְדּוֹ.	וַיַּהֲרֹג מְלָכִים אַדִּירִים
כִּי לְעוֹלָם חַסְדּוֹ.	לְסִיחוֹן מֶלֶךְ הָאֱמֹרִי
כִּי לְעוֹלָם חַסְדּוֹ.	וּלְעוֹג מֶלֶךְ הַבָּשָׁן
כִּי לְעוֹלָם חַסְדּוֹ.	וְנָתַן אַרְצָם לְנַחֲלָה
כִּי לְעוֹלָם חַסְדּוֹ.	נַחֲלָה לְיִשְׂרָאֵל עַבְדּוֹ
כִּי לְעוֹלָם חַסְדּוֹ.	שֶׁבְּשִׁפְלֵנוּ זָכַר לָנוּ

וַיִּפְרְקֵנוּ מִצָּרֵינוּ   כִּי לְעוֹלָם חַסְדּוֹ.

נָתַן לֶחֶם לְכָל בָּשָׂר   כִּי לְעוֹלָם חַסְדּוֹ.

הוֹדוּ לְאֵל הַשָּׁמָיִם   כִּי לְעוֹלָם חַסְדּוֹ.

Psalm 136

Praise the Lord for He is good,	for His grace is everlasting.
Praise the God of gods,	for His grace is everlasting.
Praise the Lord of lords,	for His grace is everlasting.
Who alone performs great miracles,	for His grace is everlasting.
Who made the heavens with wisdom,	for His grace is everlasting.
Who spread the earth over the waters,	for His grace is everlasting.
Who made the great lights,	for His grace is everlasting.
The sun to rule by day,	for His grace is everlasting.
The moon and the stars to rule by night,	for His grace is everlasting.
Who struck Egypt through their firstborn,	for His grace is everlasting.
And brought out Israel from among them,	for His grace is everlasting.
With a strong hand and outstretched arm,	for His grace is everlasting.
Who split the Red Sea,	for His grace is everlasting.
And passed Israel through it,	for His grace is everlasting.
And threw Pharaoh and his army into the Red Sea,	for His grace is everlasting.
Who led His people through the wilderness,	for His grace is everlasting.
Who struck down great kings,	for His grace is everlasting.
And slew mighty kings,	for His grace is everlasting.

Sihon, king of the Amorites,	for His grace is everlasting.
And Og, king of Bashan,	for His grace is everlasting.
And gave their land as a heritage,	for His grace is everlasting.
A heritage to His servant Israel,	for His grace is everlasting.
Who remembered us in our humiliation,	for His grace is everlasting.
And delivered us from our enemies,	for His grace is everlasting.
Who gives bread to all,	for His grace is everlasting.
Praise the God of heaven,	for His grace is everlasting.

נִשְׁמַת כָּל חַי תְּבָרֵךְ אֶת שִׁמְךָ יְיָ אֱלֹהֵינוּ, וְרוּחַ כָּל בָּשָׂר תְּפָאֵר וּתְרוֹמֵם זִכְרְךָ,

מַלְכֵּנוּ, תָּמִיד. מִן הָעוֹלָם וְעַד הָעוֹלָם אַתָּה אֵל, וּמִבַּלְעָדֶיךָ

אֵין לָנוּ מֶלֶךְ גּוֹאֵל וּמוֹשִׁיעַ, פּוֹדֶה וּמַצִּיל וּמְפַרְנֵס, וּמְרַחֵם

בְּכָל עֵת צָרָה וְצוּקָה. אֵין לָנוּ מֶלֶךְ אֶלָּא אָתָּה. אֱלֹהֵי

הָרִאשׁוֹנִים וְהָאַחֲרוֹנִים, אֱלוֹהַּ כָּל בְּרִיּוֹת. אֲדוֹן כָּל תּוֹלָדוֹת,

הַמְהֻלָּל בְּרֹב הַתִּשְׁבָּחוֹת, הַמְנַהֵג עוֹלָמוֹ בְּחֶסֶד וּבְרִיּוֹתָיו

בְּרַחֲמִים. וַיְיָ לֹא יָנוּם וְלֹא יִישָׁן, הַמְעוֹרֵר יְשֵׁנִים, וְהַמֵּקִיץ

נִרְדָּמִים, וְהַמֵּשִׂיחַ אִלְּמִים, וְהַמַּתִּיר אֲסוּרִים, וְהַסּוֹמֵךְ נוֹפְלִים,

וְהַזּוֹקֵף כְּפוּפִים, לְךָ לְבַדְּךָ אֲנַחְנוּ מוֹדִים.

אִלּוּ פִינוּ מָלֵא שִׁירָה כַיָּם, וּלְשׁוֹנֵנוּ רִנָּה כַּהֲמוֹן גַּלָּיו,

וְשִׂפְתוֹתֵינוּ שֶׁבַח כְּמֶרְחֲבֵי רָקִיעַ, וְעֵינֵינוּ מְאִירוֹת כַּשֶּׁמֶשׁ
וְכַיָּרֵחַ, וְיָדֵינוּ פְרוּשׂוֹת כְּנִשְׁרֵי שָׁמָיִם, וְרַגְלֵינוּ קַלּוֹת
כָּאַיָּלוֹת, אֵין אֲנַחְנוּ מַסְפִּיקִים לְהוֹדוֹת לְךָ, יְיָ אֱלֹהֵינוּ וֵאלֹהֵי
אֲבוֹתֵינוּ, וּלְבָרֵךְ אֶת שְׁמֶךָ עַל אַחַת מֵאֶלֶף אֶלֶף אַלְפֵי
אֲלָפִים וְרִבֵּי רְבָבוֹת פְּעָמִים הַטּוֹבוֹת שֶׁעָשִׂיתָ עִם אֲבוֹתֵינוּ
וְעִמָּנוּ. מִמִּצְרַיִם גְּאַלְתָּנוּ יְיָ אֱלֹהֵינוּ וּמִבֵּית עֲבָדִים פְּדִיתָנוּ,
בְּרָעָב זַנְתָּנוּ וּבְשָׂבָע כִּלְכַּלְתָּנוּ; מֵחֶרֶב הִצַּלְתָּנוּ וּמִדֶּבֶר
מִלַּטְתָּנוּ, וּמֵחֳלָיִם רָעִים וְנֶאֱמָנִים דִּלִּיתָנוּ. עַד הֵנָּה עֲזָרוּנוּ
רַחֲמֶיךָ וְלֹא עֲזָבוּנוּ חֲסָדֶיךָ; וְאַל תִּטְּשֵׁנוּ יְיָ אֱלֹהֵינוּ לָנֶצַח.
עַל כֵּן, אֵבָרִים שֶׁפִּלַּגְתָּ בָּנוּ, וְרוּחַ וּנְשָׁמָה שֶׁנָּפַחְתָּ בְּאַפֵּינוּ,
וְלָשׁוֹן אֲשֶׁר שַׂמְתָּ בְּפִינוּ, הֵן הֵם יוֹדוּ וִיבָרְכוּ, וִישַׁבְּחוּ וִיפָאֲרוּ,
וִירוֹמְמוּ וְיַעֲרִיצוּ, וְיַקְדִּישׁוּ וְיַמְלִיכוּ אֶת שִׁמְךָ, מַלְכֵּנוּ. כִּי כָל
פֶּה לְךָ יוֹדֶה, וְכָל לָשׁוֹן לְךָ תִשָּׁבַע, וְכָל בֶּרֶךְ לְךָ תִכְרַע,
וְכָל קוֹמָה לְפָנֶיךָ תִשְׁתַּחֲוֶה. וְכָל לְבָבוֹת יִירָאוּךָ, וְכָל קֶרֶב
וּכְלָיוֹת יְזַמְּרוּ לִשְׁמֶךָ, כַּדָּבָר שֶׁכָּתוּב: כָּל עַצְמֹתַי תֹּאמַרְנָה,
יְיָ מִי כָמוֹךָ, מַצִּיל עָנִי מֵחָזָק מִמֶּנּוּ, וְעָנִי וְאֶבְיוֹן מִגֹּזְלוֹ. מִי
יִדְמֶה לָּךְ, וּמִי יִשְׁוֶה לָּךְ, וּמִי יַעֲרָךְ-לָךְ, הָאֵל הַגָּדוֹל הַגִּבּוֹר

וְהַנּוֹרָא אֵל עֶלְיוֹן קֹנֵה שָׁמַיִם וָאָרֶץ. נְהַלֶּלְךָ וּנְשַׁבֵּחֲךָ וּנְפָאֶרְךָ, וּנְבָרֵךְ אֶת שֵׁם קָדְשֶׁךָ, כָּאָמוּר: לְדָוִד, בָּרְכִי נַפְשִׁי, אֶת יְיָ, וְכָל קְרָבַי אֶת שֵׁם קָדְשׁוֹ.

הָאֵל בְּתַעֲצֻמוֹת עֻזֶּךָ, הַגָּדוֹל בִּכְבוֹד שְׁמֶךָ, הַגִּבּוֹר לָנֶצַח וְהַנּוֹרָא בְּנוֹרְאוֹתֶיךָ, הַמֶּלֶךְ הַיּוֹשֵׁב עַל כִּסֵּא רָם וְנִשָּׂא.

שׁוֹכֵן עַד, מָרוֹם וְקָדוֹשׁ שְׁמוֹ. וְכָתוּב: רַנְּנוּ צַדִּיקִים בַּיְיָ, לַיְשָׁרִים נָאוָה תְהִלָּה. בְּפִי יְשָׁרִים תִּתְהַלָּל, וּבְדִבְרֵי צַדִּיקִים תִּתְבָּרַךְ, וּבִלְשׁוֹן חֲסִידִים תִּתְרוֹמָם, וּבְקֶרֶב קְדוֹשִׁים תִּתְקַדָּשׁ.

וּבְמַקְהֲלוֹת רִבְבוֹת עַמְּךָ בֵּית יִשְׂרָאֵל בְּרִנָּה יִתְפָּאַר שִׁמְךָ, מַלְכֵּנוּ, בְּכָל דּוֹר וָדוֹר. שֶׁכֵּן חוֹבַת כָּל הַיְצוּרִים לְפָנֶיךָ, יְיָ אֱלֹהֵינוּ וֵאלֹהֵי אֲבוֹתֵינוּ, לְהוֹדוֹת, לְהַלֵּל, לְשַׁבֵּחַ, לְפָאֵר, לְרוֹמֵם, לְהַדֵּר, לְבָרֵךְ, לְעַלֵּה וּלְקַלֵּס עַל כָּל דִּבְרֵי שִׁירוֹת וְתִשְׁבְּחוֹת דָּוִד בֶּן־יִשַׁי עַבְדְּךָ, מְשִׁיחֶךָ.

יִשְׁתַּבַּח שִׁמְךָ לָעַד, מַלְכֵּנוּ, הָאֵל הַמֶּלֶךְ הַגָּדוֹל וְהַקָּדוֹשׁ, בַּשָּׁמַיִם וּבָאָרֶץ. כִּי לְךָ נָאֶה, יְיָ אֱלֹהֵינוּ וֵאלֹהֵי אֲבוֹתֵינוּ, שִׁיר

וּשְׁבָחָה, הַלֵּל וְזִמְרָה, עֹז וּמֶמְשָׁלָה, נֶצַח, גְּדֻלָּה וּגְבוּרָה, תְּהִלָּה

וְתִפְאֶרֶת, קְדֻשָּׁה וּמַלְכוּת, בְּרָכוֹת וְהוֹדָאוֹת, מֵעַתָּה וְעַד

עוֹלָם. בָּרוּךְ אַתָּה יְיָ, אֵל מֶלֶךְ גָּדוֹל בַּתִּשְׁבָּחוֹת, אֵל

הַהוֹדָאוֹת, אֲדוֹן הַנִּפְלָאוֹת, הַבּוֹחֵר בְּשִׁירֵי זִמְרָה, מֶלֶךְ, אֵל,

חֵי הָעוֹלָמִים.

Nishmat, a prayer

The soul of all the living praises Your name.
The spirit of all that is flesh glorifies and exalts the memory of
    Your name.
In times of distress and oppression, You alone are our King.
You are God first and God last, God of all the living.
You rule Your world with grace and its creatures with compassion.
You, God, do not close Your eyes, nor do You sleep.
You awaken those who sleep and You awaken those who slumber.
You give speech to the mute.
You free those in prison.
You support those who have fallen and You Help those who are
    bowed down.
To You alone we are grateful.
If our mouths were full of praise, as full as the sea,
If our tongues could sing the way the waves are singing,
If our lips could exalt You the way the heavens do,
If our eyes could shine like the sun and the moon,
If our arms could be outstretched like the eagles under the sky,
If our feet could be as swift as the gazelle's,
Even then, we would not be capable of thanking You, God of our
    fathers and fathers' fathers, and bless Your name

For all the thousands, and thousands of thousands, and tens of thousands of the blessings that You have offered our ancestors and ourselves.

You have redeemed us from Egypt, God.

You have taken us out of bondage.

You have fed us when we were hungry and in times of plenty You sustained us.

You saved us from the sword.

You helped us overcome pestilence.

You cured us from disease.

You were always there when we needed You.

Until now, Your grace was with us and Your compassion did not abandon us.

So, please do not abandon us, ever.

So, all the limbs You have fashioned and the spirit and soul You have breathed into us, and the tongue You have placed in our mouth—

All thank You and exalt You and glorify You, and hallow and sanctify Your name, our Lord.

For every mouth thanks You, every tongue swears allegiance to You.

Every knee bends to You, everyone standing prostrates himself before You and all hearts fear You.

All Your creatures sing Your glory as it is written: "All my bones say,

'Who can be compared to You, God.

You save the poor from those who are stronger, and You save the beggar from the thief who tries to defeat him.' "

Who is like You?

Who can be compared to You?

Who can come near You in Your grandeur?

You are the God, the Great, the Mighty, the Awesome, the Supreme God. The Ruler of heaven and earth. We shall praise You and glorify You and bless Your holy name as it is written in David's name:

"O my soul, bless God, and all my being, bless His holy name."

God, in Your glory and Your strength
God, whose name means eternal strength.
God, who sits on the throne, both mighty and exalted.

God, who dwells eternally, exalted and holy is Your name.
As it is written: "Rejoice in God, you righteous; it is fit that the
    righteous sing His praise."
On the lips of the righteous, You will be praised.
In the words of the just, You have been blessed.
By the tongue of the pious, You have been exalted.
And in the midst of the holy, Your sanctity will remain sanctified.

In the assemblies of the multitudes of Your people of Israel, Your
name, our King, will be glorified from generation to generation.
For it is the obligation of all Your creatures, Lord our God, God of
our forefathers, to thank You, to praise You, to glorify You, to
elevate You, to exalt You, and to extol You. In the words of the
Songs and the Psalms that David, son of Yishai, Your anointed
king, has already used, and we can only repeat:

Praised be Your name, King, God of greatness and holiness in
heaven and earth. For to You God, God of our fathers and forefathers, it is befitting to offer praise and song. Expressing Your
strength, Your justice, Your eternity, Your holiness and all the
blessings and thanksgivings we owe You, now, until the end of all
time. Blessed are You, God, King, great in praises, God to whom
our thanks are due, Lord of wonders, who delights in songs and
hymns, King, God, life of the Universe.

*After saying the blessing we drink the fourth cup of wine while
reclining.*

בָּרוּךְ אַתָּה יְיָ אֱלֹהֵינוּ מֶלֶךְ הָעוֹלָם בּוֹרֵא פְּרִי הַגָּפֶן.

Blessed are You, Lord our God, King of the Universe, who creates the fruit of the vine.

On the Sabbath, add bracketed words.

בָּרוּךְ אַתָּה יְיָ אֱלֹהֵינוּ מֶלֶךְ הָעוֹלָם, עַל הַגֶּפֶן וְעַל פְּרִי הַגֶּפֶן, וְעַל תְּנוּבַת הַשָּׂדֶה, וְעַל אֶרֶץ חֶמְדָּה טוֹבָה וּרְחָבָה שֶׁרָצִיתָ וְהִנְחַלְתָּ לַאֲבוֹתֵינוּ לֶאֱכֹל מִפִּרְיָהּ וְלִשְׂבֹּעַ מִטּוּבָהּ. רַחֶם נָא יְיָ אֱלֹהֵינוּ עַל יִשְׂרָאֵל עַמֶּךָ, וְעַל יְרוּשָׁלַיִם עִירֶךָ, וְעַל צִיּוֹן מִשְׁכַּן כְּבוֹדֶךָ, וְעַל מִזְבַּחֶךָ וְעַל הֵיכָלֶךָ. וּבְנֵה יְרוּשָׁלַיִם עִיר הַקֹּדֶשׁ בִּמְהֵרָה בְיָמֵינוּ, וְהַעֲלֵנוּ לְתוֹכָהּ וְשַׂמְּחֵנוּ בְּבִנְיָנָהּ, וְנֹאכַל מִפִּרְיָהּ וְנִשְׂבַּע מִטּוּבָהּ, וּנְבָרֶכְךָ עָלֶיהָ בִּקְדֻשָּׁה וּבְטָהֳרָה. (וּרְצֵה וְהַחֲלִיצֵנוּ בְּיוֹם הַשַּׁבָּת הַזֶּה.) וְשַׂמְּחֵנוּ בְּיוֹם חַג הַמַּצּוֹת הַזֶּה. כִּי אַתָּה, יְיָ, טוֹב וּמֵטִיב לַכֹּל, וְנוֹדֶה לְךָ עַל הָאָרֶץ וְעַל פְּרִי הַגָּפֶן. בָּרוּךְ אַתָּה יְיָ עַל הָאָרֶץ וְעַל פְּרִי הַגָּפֶן.

117

Blessed are You, Lord our God, King of the Universe, for the vine, and for the fruit of the vine, and for the produce of the field, and for the desirable, good, and spacious land which in Your love You gave our fathers as an inheritance to eat its fruits and enjoy its harvests. Have mercy, Lord our God, on Israel Your people and Jerusalem Your city, on Zion the home of Your glory, on Your altar, and on Your Temple. Rebuild Jerusalem the holy city, soon and in our day, and lead us there and let us rejoice in its rebuilding. And may we eat its fruits and enjoy its blessings and praise You in holiness and purity. [Favor and strengthen us on this Sabbath day.] And may we rejoice on this day the festival of matzah. For You, Lord, are good, and are kind to all, and so we thank You for the land and for the fruit of the vine. Blessed are You, Lord, for the land and for the fruit of the vine.

נִרְצָה

Nirtzah

CONCLUSION OF THE SERVICE

חֲסַל סְדּוּר פֶּסַח כְּהִלְכָתוֹ, כְּכָל מִשְׁפָּטוֹ וְחֻקָּתוֹ. כַּאֲשֶׁר זָכִינוּ לְסַדֵּר אוֹתוֹ, כֵּן נִזְכֶּה לַעֲשׂוֹתוֹ. זָךְ שׁוֹכֵן מְעוֹנָה, קוֹמֵם קְהַל עֲדַת מִי מָנָה. בְּקָרוֹב נַהֵל נִטְעֵי כַנָּה, פְּדוּיִים לְצִיּוֹן בְּרִנָּה.

And so we end the Passover Seder.
We have conducted it according to custom, according to law.
Just as we have been privileged to celebrate it this year,
    may we be worthy of performing it in the future as well.
Pure One, God in Purity, and Oneness in heaven,
    restore Your countless people.
Speedily lead us redeemed to Zion in joy.

לְשָׁנָה הַבָּאָה בִּירוּשָׁלָיִם!

NEXT YEAR IN JERUSALEM!

This article of faith, this song of hope which reverberates from century to century, from country to country, from exile to exile, from massacre to massacre, is restated here tonight. Jews are being murdered again? Next year the killing will stop. Jews are again being starved and persecuted? Next year, the story of their persecution will be told. Always next year. Next year in Jerusalem. But today in Jerusalem, when Jews reach this place in the Haggadah, they recite the phrase with one difference: "Next year in a rebuilt Jerusalem!"

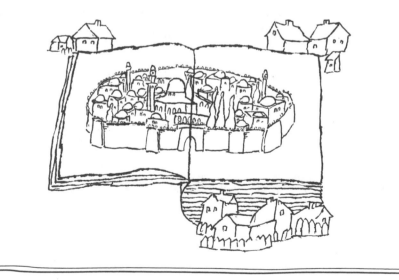

COUNTING THE OMER
Recited on the second Seder night

At the end of the second Seder, we begin the count-down of the forty-nine days until Shavuot, which celebrates the revelation at Sinai. These seven weeks are known as the days of the Omer. During these seven weeks, weddings and haircuts are prohibited in deference to the mourning for the plague that decimated the disciples of Rabbi Akiba. Our sages tell us that in the era of the Temple, there was an Omer offering in repayment for the manna which fell in the wilderness. Only on the thirty-third day, Lag

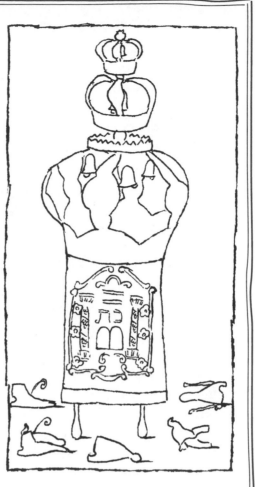

B'Omer, when the plague ceased, are the bans lifted. The mystics attach a different significance to Lag B'Omer: It was the day the great sage Shimon bar Yochai died, and on his death, many secrets were revealed to his disciples. And so bonfires are lit to celebrate the great light that once filled the world on that day.

בָּרוּךְ אַתָּה יְיָ אֱלֹהֵינוּ מֶלֶךְ הָעוֹלָם אֲשֶׁר
קִדְּשָׁנוּ בְּמִצְוֹתָיו וְצִוָּנוּ עַל סְפִירַת הָעוֹמֶר.

Blessed are You, Lord our God, King of the Universe, who has sanctified us with His laws and commanded us to count the Omer.

הַיּוֹם יוֹם אֶחָד לָעוֹמֶר.

Today is the first day of the Omer.

Now that the story has been told and praise and thanks have been given, the last part of the Seder will be devoted to singing.

The songs are simple and touchingly naive. We sing them to make a point: The Haggadah is not just a story—it is also a melody.

Recited on the first Seder night.

וּבְכֵן וַיְהִי בַּחֲצִי הַלַּיְלָה

אָז רוֹב נִסִּים הִפְלֵאתָ בַּלַּיְלָה,

בְּרֹאשׁ אַשְׁמוּרוֹת זֶה הַלַּיְלָה,

גֵּר צֶדֶק נִצַּחְתּוֹ כְּנֶחֱלַק לוֹ לַיְלָה.

וַיְהִי בַּחֲצִי הַלַּיְלָה.

דַּנְתָּ מֶלֶךְ גְּרָר בַּחֲלוֹם הַלַּיְלָה,

הִפְחַדְתָּ אֲרַמִּי בְּאֶמֶשׁ לַיְלָה,

וַיִּשַּׂר יִשְׂרָאֵל לְמַלְאָךְ וַיּוּכַל לוֹ לַיְלָה.

121

וַיְהִי בַּחֲצִי הַלַּיְלָה.

זֶרַע בְּכוֹרֵי פַתְרוֹס מָחַצְתָּ בַּחֲצִי הַלַּיְלָה,

חֵילָם לֹא מָצְאוּ בְּקוּמָם בַּלַּיְלָה,

טִיסַת נְגִיד חֲרֹשֶׁת סִלִּיתָ בְּכוֹכְבֵי לַיְלָה.

וַיְהִי בַּחֲצִי הַלַּיְלָה.

יָעַץ מְחָרֵף לְנוֹפֵף אִוּוּי הוֹבַשְׁתָּ פְגָרָיו בַּלַּיְלָה,

כָּרַע בֵּל וּמַצָּבוֹ בְּאִישׁוֹן לַיְלָה,

לְאִישׁ חֲמוּדוֹת נִגְלָה רָז חֲזוֹת לַיְלָה.

וַיְהִי בַּחֲצִי הַלַּיְלָה.

מִשְׁתַּכֵּר בִּכְלֵי קֹדֶשׁ נֶהֱרַג בּוֹ בַּלַּיְלָה,

נוֹשַׁע מִבּוֹר אֲרָיוֹת פּוֹתֵר בְּעָתוּתֵי לַיְלָה,

שִׂנְאָה נָטַר אֲגָגִי וְכָתַב סְפָרִים בַּלַּיְלָה,

וַיְהִי בַּחֲצִי הַלַּיְלָה.

עוֹרַרְתָּ נִצְחֲךָ עָלָיו בְּנֶדֶד שְׁנַת לַיְלָה,

פּוּרָה תִדְרוֹךְ לְשׁוֹמֵר מַה מִלַּיְלָה,

צָרַח כַּשׁוֹמֵר וְשָׂח אָתָא בֹקֶר וְגַם לַיְלָה.

וַיְהִי בַּחֲצִי הַלַּיְלָה.

קָרֵב יוֹם אֲשֶׁר הוּא לֹא יוֹם וְלֹא לַיְלָה,

רָם הוֹדַע כִּי לְךָ הַיּוֹם אַף לְךָ הַלַּיְלָה,

שׁוֹמְרִים הַפְקֵד לְעִירְךָ כָּל הַיּוֹם וְכָל הַלַּיְלָה,

תָּאִיר כְּאוֹר יוֹם חֶשְׁכַת לַיְלָה.

וַיְהִי בַּחֲצִי הַלַּיְלָה.

And It Happened At Midnight

Most of the miracles You performed occurred at night.
At the beginning of the watch of this very night.
Abraham achieved his victory when he divided his family at night.
It happened at midnight.

You judged Abimelech, the Philistine King of Gerar, in a dream at
   night.
You frightened Laban the Aramaean at night.
Israel wrestled with God and vanquished His angel at night.
It happened at midnight.

You struck down the firstborn of Egypt at night.
The Egyptians found their strength gone when they arose at night.
The army of Sisera was defeated by You at night.
It happened at midnight.

The Assyrian armies, under Sennacherib, besieging Jerusalem,
   were defeated at night.
Bel and his pedestal were overthrown at night.
You revealed Your mysteries to Daniel at night.
It happened at midnight.

King Belshazzar of Babylon became drunk when he drank from
   the holy vessels and was slain at night.

Daniel was safe in the lion's den and interpreted the dreams of
   terror at night.
Haman wrote his decree of hate at night.
It all happened at midnight.

You prevailed over Haman by disturbing the sleep of Ahasuerus at
   night.
You will crush the wicked like grapes in a wine press for those
   who ask, "When will there be an end to night?"
And like the watchman, may we all cry out, "The morning has
   come, as did night."
It always happened at midnight.

May the day arrive, a continuous day, neither day nor night.
God, make known Your will and Your desire that the day is Yours
   as is night.
Appoint guards over Your city all day and all night.
Brighten as the light of the day the darkness of the night.
All miracles occurred at midnight.

Recited on the second Seder night.

וּבְכֵן וַאֲמַרְתֶּם זֶבַח פֶּסַח

אֹמֶץ גְּבוּרוֹתֶיךָ הִפְלֵאתָ בַּפֶּסַח,

בְּרֹאשׁ כָּל מוֹעֲדוֹת נִשֵּׂאתָ פֶּסַח,

גִּלִּיתָ לְאֶזְרָחִי חֲצוֹת לֵיל פֶּסַח.

וַאֲמַרְתֶּם זֶבַח פֶּסַח.   דְּלָתָיו דָּפַקְתָּ כְּחֹם הַיּוֹם בַּפֶּסַח,

הִסְעִיד נוֹצְצִים עֻגוֹת מַצּוֹת בַּפֶּסַח,

124

וְאֶל הַבָּקָר רָץ זֵכֶר לְשׁוֹר עֵרֶךְ פֶּסַח.　וַאֲמַרְתֶּם זֶבַח פֶּסַח.

זֹעֲמוּ סְדוֹמִים וְלֹהֲטוּ בָּאֵשׁ בַּפֶּסַח,

חֻלַּץ לוֹט מֵהֶם וּמַצּוֹת אָפָה בְּקֵץ פֶּסַח,

טֵאטֵאתָ אַדְמַת מֹף וְנֹף בְּעָבְרְךָ בַּפֶּסַח.

וַאֲמַרְתֶּם זֶבַח פֶּסַח.

יָהּ רֹאשׁ כָּל אוֹן מָחַצְתָּ בְּלֵיל שְׁמוּר פֶּסַח,

כַּבִּיר עַל בֵּן בְּכוֹר פָּסַחְתָּ בְּדַם פֶּסַח,

לְבִלְתִּי תֵּת מַשְׁחִית לָבֹא בִּפְתָחַי בַּפֶּסַח.

וַאֲמַרְתֶּם זֶבַח פֶּסַח.

מְסֻגֶּרֶת סֻגְּרָה בְּעִתּוֹתֵי פֶּסַח,

נִשְׁמְדָה מִדְיָן בִּצְלִיל שְׂעוֹרֵי עֹמֶר פֶּסַח,

שֹׂרְפוּ מִשְׁמַנֵּי פוּל וְלוּד בִּיקַד יְקוֹד פֶּסַח.

וַאֲמַרְתֶּם זֶבַח פֶּסַח.

עוֹד הַיּוֹם בְּנֹב לַעֲמֹד עַד גָּעָה עוֹנַת פֶּסַח,

פַּס יָד כָּתְבָה לְקַעֲקֵעַ צוּל בַּפֶּסַח,

צָפֹה הַצָּפִית עָרֹךְ הַשֻּׁלְחָן בַּפֶּסַח.　וַאֲמַרְתֶּם זֶבַח פֶּסַח.

קָהָל כִּנְּסָה הֲדַסָּה צוֹם לְשַׁלֵּשׁ בַּפֶּסַח,

125

רֹאשׁ מִבֵּית רָשָׁע מָחַצְתָּ בְּעֵץ חֲמִשִּׁים בַּפֶּסַח,

שְׁתֵּי אֵלֶּה רֶגַע תָּבִיא לְעוּצִית בַּפֶּסַח,

תָּעֹז יָדְךָ תָּרוּם יְמִינְךָ כְּלֵיל הִתְקַדֶּשׁ חַג פֶּסַח.

וַאֲמַרְתֶּם זֶבַח פֶּסַח.

This Is the Festival of Passover

You revealed Your great power on Passover.
You placed above all festivals Passover.
You revealed Yourself to Abraham at midnight on Passover.
This is the festival of Passover.

In the heat of the day, You knocked on Abraham's door on
    Passover.
He fed the angels cakes of unleavened bread on Passover.
And he ran to the herd to offer a calf on Passover.
This is the festival of Passover.

The men and women in Sodom provoked God and were
    consumed by fire on Passover.
Lot was saved and he baked unleavened bread on Passover.
Egypt was swept away when You passed through it on Passover.
This is the festival of Passover.

You killed the firstborn on the night of Passover.
You spared Israel's firstborn on Passover.
The destroyer was not allowed to enter Israel's doors on Passover.
This is the festival of Passover.

The walls of Jericho fell on Passover.
Through a dream of barley cake, the land of Midian was destroyed
    on Passover.

The princes of Pul and Lud were burned in a mighty fire on
  Passover.
This is the festival of Passover.

King Sennacherib met disaster while preparing to attack Jerusalem
  on Passover.
The hand wrote the warning on the wall of Babylon on Passover.
Just when the table was spread and all arranged on Passover.
This is the festival of Passover.

Queen Esther gathered her people to fast three days on Passover.
Haman was hanged on the gallows on Passover.
Double punishment will be inflicted on our enemies by You on
  Passover.
May Your mighty right hand bring our final redemption on
  Passover.
This is the festival of Passover.

כִּי לוֹ נָאֶה כִּי לוֹ יָאֶה

אַדִּיר בִּמְלוּכָה, בָּחוּר כַּהֲלָכָה, גְּדוּדָיו יֹאמְרוּ לוֹ:

לְךָ וּלְךָ, לְךָ כִּי לְךָ, לְךָ אַף לְךָ, לְךָ יְיָ הַמַּמְלָכָה.

כִּי לוֹ נָאֶה, כִּי לוֹ יָאֶה.

דָּגוּל בִּמְלוּכָה, הָדוּר כַּהֲלָכָה, וָתִיקָיו יֹאמְרוּ לוֹ:

לְךָ וּלְךָ, לְךָ כִּי לְךָ, לְךָ אַף לְךָ, לְךָ יְיָ הַמַּמְלָכָה.

כִּי לוֹ נָאֶה, כִּי לוֹ יָאֶה.

זַכַּאי בִּמְלוּכָה, חָסִין כַּהֲלָכָה, טַפְסְרָיו יֹאמְרוּ לוֹ:

לְךָ וּלְךָ, לְךָ כִּי לְךָ, לְךָ אַף לְךָ, לְךָ יְיָ הַמַּמְלָכָה.

כִּי לוֹ נָאֶה, כִּי לוֹ יָאֶה.

יָחִיד בִּמְלוּכָה, כַּבִּיר כַּהֲלָכָה, לִמּוּדָיו יֹאמְרוּ לוֹ:

לְךָ וּלְךָ, לְךָ כִּי לְךָ, לְךָ אַף לְךָ, לְךָ יְיָ הַמַּמְלָכָה.

כִּי לוֹ נָאֶה, כִּי לוֹ יָאֶה.

מוֹשֵׁל בִּמְלוּכָה, נוֹרָא כַּהֲלָכָה, סְבִיבָיו יֹאמְרוּ לוֹ:

לְךָ וּלְךָ, לְךָ כִּי לְךָ, לְךָ אַף לְךָ, לְךָ יְיָ הַמַּמְלָכָה.

כִּי לוֹ נָאֶה, כִּי לוֹ יָאֶה.

עָנָו בִּמְלוּכָה, פּוֹדֶה כַּהֲלָכָה, צַדִּיקָיו יֹאמְרוּ לוֹ:

לְךָ וּלְךָ, לְךָ כִּי לְךָ, לְךָ אַף לְךָ, לְךָ יְיָ הַמַּמְלָכָה.

כִּי לוֹ נָאֶה, כִּי לוֹ יָאֶה.

קָדוֹשׁ בִּמְלוּכָה, רַחוּם כַּהֲלָכָה, שִׁנְאַנָּיו יֹאמְרוּ לוֹ:

לְךָ וּלְךָ, לְךָ כִּי לְךָ, לְךָ אַף לְךָ, לְךָ יְיָ הַמַּמְלָכָה.

כִּי לוֹ נָאֶה, כִּי לוֹ יָאֶה.

תַּקִּיף בִּמְלוּכָה, תּוֹמֵךְ כַּהֲלָכָה, תְּמִימָיו יֹאמְרוּ לוֹ:

לְךָ וּלְךָ, לְךָ כִּי לְךָ, לְךָ אַף לְךָ, לְךָ יְיָ הַמַּמְלָכָה.

כִּי לוֹ נָאֶה, כִּי לוֹ יָאֶה.

All Praises Are His, All Praises Are Due Him

Mighty in majesty, truly chosen, His angels sing to Him:
Yours alone is the world, God. For all in the world is Yours.
All praises are His, all praises are due Him.

Distinguished in majesty, truly glorious, those who believe in Him
   sing to Him:
Yours alone is the world, God. For all in the world is Yours.
All praises are His, all praises are due Him.

Pure in majesty, truly powerful, those who attend to Him sing to
   Him:
Yours alone is the world, God. For all in the world is Yours.
All praises are His, all praises are due Him.

Unique in majesty, truly mighty, those who learn from Him sing
   to Him:
Yours alone is the world, God. For all in the world is Yours.
All praises are His, all praises are due Him.

Ruling Creation in majesty, He is truly revered. All that surround
   Him sing to Him:
Yours alone is the world, God. For all in the world is Yours.
All praises are His, all praises are due Him.

Humble in majesty, truly redeeming, the righteous who claim their
   obedience to Him sing to Him:
Yours alone is the world, God. For all in the world is Yours.
All praises are His, all praises are due Him.

Holy in majesty, truly compassionate, His multitudes sing to Him:
Yours alone is the world, God. For all in the world is Yours.
All praises are His, all praises are due Him.

Almighty in majesty, truly sustaining, the innocent sing their in-
   nocence to Him:
Yours alone is the world, God. For all in the world is Yours.
All praises are His, all praises are due Him.

אַדִּיר הוּא

אַדִּיר הוּא, יִבְנֶה בֵיתוֹ בְּקָרוֹב,

בִּמְהֵרָה בִּמְהֵרָה בְּיָמֵינוּ בְּקָרוֹב,

אֵל בְּנֵה, אֵל בְּנֵה, בְּנֵה בֵיתְךָ בְּקָרוֹב.

בָּחוּר הוּא, גָּדוֹל הוּא, דָּגוּל הוּא, יִבְנֶה בֵיתוֹ בְּקָרוֹב,

בִּמְהֵרָה בִּמְהֵרָה בְּיָמֵינוּ בְּקָרוֹב,

אֵל בְּנֵה, אֵל בְּנֵה, בְּנֵה בֵיתְךָ בְּקָרוֹב.

הָדוּר הוּא, וָתִיק הוּא, זַכַּאי הוּא, יִבְנֶה בֵיתוֹ בְּקָרוֹב,

בִּמְהֵרָה בִּמְהֵרָה בְּיָמֵינוּ בְּקָרוֹב,

אֵל בְּנֵה, אֵל בְּנֵה, בְּנֵה בֵיתְךָ בְּקָרוֹב.

חָסִיד הוּא, טָהוֹר הוּא, יָחִיד הוּא, יִבְנֶה בֵיתוֹ בְּקָרוֹב,

בִּמְהֵרָה בִּמְהֵרָה בְּיָמֵינוּ בְּקָרוֹב,

אֵל בְּנֵה, אֵל בְּנֵה, בְּנֵה בֵיתְךָ בְּקָרוֹב.

כַּבִּיר הוּא, לָמוּד הוּא, מֶלֶךְ הוּא, יִבְנֶה בֵיתוֹ בְּקָרוֹב,

בִּמְהֵרָה בִּמְהֵרָה בְּיָמֵינוּ בְּקָרוֹב,

אֵל בְּנֵה, אֵל בְּנֵה, בְּנֵה בֵיתְךָ בְּקָרוֹב.

נוֹרָא הוּא, סַגִּיב הוּא, עִזּוּז הוּא, יִבְנֶה בֵיתוֹ בְּקָרוֹב,

בִּמְהֵרָה בִּמְהֵרָה בְּיָמֵינוּ בְּקָרוֹב,

אֵל בְּנֵה, אֵל בְּנֵה, בְּנֵה בֵיתְךָ בְּקָרוֹב.

פּוֹדֶה הוּא, צַדִּיק הוּא, קָדוֹשׁ הוּא, יִבְנֶה בֵיתוֹ בְּקָרוֹב,

בִּמְהֵרָה בִּמְהֵרָה בְּיָמֵינוּ בְּקָרוֹב,

אֵל בְּנֵה, אֵל בְּנֵה, בְּנֵה בֵיתְךָ בְּקָרוֹב.

רַחוּם הוּא, שַׁדַּי הוּא, תַּקִּיף הוּא, יִבְנֶה בֵיתוֹ בְּקָרוֹב,

בִּמְהֵרָה בִּמְהֵרָה בְּיָמֵינוּ בְּקָרוֹב,

אֵל בְּנֵה, אֵל בְּנֵה, בְּנֵה בֵיתְךָ בְּקָרוֹב.

How mighty is God.

May He rebuild His Temple, speedily, speedily in our own days,
    soon, very soon, God, do redeem, do rebuild Your House soon.

God is chosen. God is great. God is hallowed.

May He rebuild His Temple, speedily . . .

God is glorious. God is ancient. God is just.

May He rebuild His Temple, speedily . . .

God is pious. God is pure. God is unique.

May He rebuild His Temple, speedily . . .

God is colossal. God is learned. God is royal.

May He rebuild His Temple, speedily . . .

God is awesome. God is strong. God is powerful.

May He rebuild His Temple, speedily . . .

God is redeeming. God is righteous. God is holy.

May He rebuild His Temple, speedily . . .

God is merciful. God is the Almighty. God is irresistible.

May He rebuild His Temple, speedily . . .

אֶחָד מִי יוֹדֵעַ

אֶחָד מִי יוֹדֵעַ? אֶחָד אֲנִי יוֹדֵעַ:

אֶחָד אֱלֹהֵינוּ שֶׁבַּשָּׁמַיִם וּבָאָרֶץ.

שְׁנַיִם מִי יוֹדֵעַ? שְׁנַיִם אֲנִי יוֹדֵעַ:

שְׁנֵי לֻחוֹת הַבְּרִית,

אֶחָד אֱלֹהֵינוּ שֶׁבַּשָּׁמַיִם וּבָאָרֶץ.

שְׁלֹשָׁה מִי יוֹדֵעַ? שְׁלֹשָׁה אֲנִי יוֹדֵעַ:

שְׁלֹשָׁה אָבוֹת, שְׁנֵי לֻחוֹת הַבְּרִית,

אֶחָד אֱלֹהֵינוּ שֶׁבַּשָּׁמַיִם וּבָאָרֶץ.

אַרְבַּע מִי יוֹדֵעַ? אַרְבַּע אֲנִי יוֹדֵעַ:

אַרְבַּע אִמָּהוֹת, שְׁלוֹשָׁה אָבוֹת, שְׁנֵי לֻחוֹת הַבְּרִית,

אֶחָד אֱלֹהֵינוּ שֶׁבַּשָּׁמַיִם וּבָאָרֶץ.

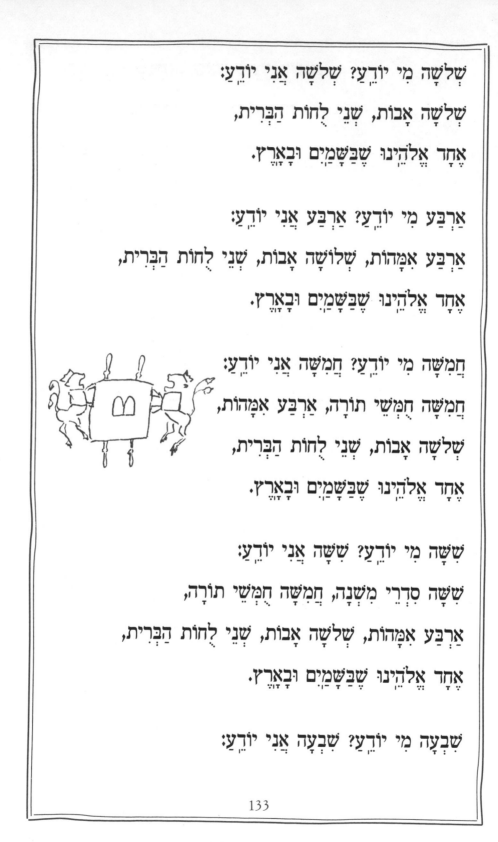

חֲמִשָּׁה מִי יוֹדֵעַ? חֲמִשָּׁה אֲנִי יוֹדֵעַ:

חֲמִשָּׁה חֻמְשֵׁי תוֹרָה, אַרְבַּע אִמָּהוֹת,

שְׁלֹשָׁה אָבוֹת, שְׁנֵי לֻחוֹת הַבְּרִית,

אֶחָד אֱלֹהֵינוּ שֶׁבַּשָּׁמַיִם וּבָאָרֶץ.

שִׁשָּׁה מִי יוֹדֵעַ? שִׁשָּׁה אֲנִי יוֹדֵעַ:

שִׁשָּׁה סִדְרֵי מִשְׁנָה, חֲמִשָּׁה חֻמְשֵׁי תוֹרָה,

אַרְבַּע אִמָּהוֹת, שְׁלֹשָׁה אָבוֹת, שְׁנֵי לֻחוֹת הַבְּרִית,

אֶחָד אֱלֹהֵינוּ שֶׁבַּשָּׁמַיִם וּבָאָרֶץ.

שִׁבְעָה מִי יוֹדֵעַ? שִׁבְעָה אֲנִי יוֹדֵעַ:

שִׁבְעָה יְמֵי שַׁבַּתָּא, שִׁשָּׁה סִדְרֵי מִשְׁנָה,

חֲמִשָּׁה חֻמְשֵׁי תוֹרָה, אַרְבַּע אִמָּהוֹת,

שְׁלֹשָׁה אָבוֹת, שְׁנֵי לֻחוֹת הַבְּרִית,

אֶחָד אֱלֹהֵינוּ שֶׁבַּשָּׁמַיִם וּבָאָרֶץ.

שְׁמוֹנָה מִי יוֹדֵעַ? שְׁמוֹנָה אֲנִי יוֹדֵעַ:

שְׁמוֹנָה יְמֵי מִילָה, שִׁבְעָה יְמֵי שַׁבַּתָּא,

שִׁשָּׁה סִדְרֵי מִשְׁנָה, חֲמִשָּׁה חֻמְשֵׁי תוֹרָה,

אַרְבַּע אִמָּהוֹת, שְׁלֹשָׁה אָבוֹת, שְׁנֵי לֻחוֹת הַבְּרִית,

אֶחָד אֱלֹהֵינוּ שֶׁבַּשָּׁמַיִם וּבָאָרֶץ.

תִּשְׁעָה מִי יוֹדֵעַ? תִּשְׁעָה אֲנִי יוֹדֵעַ:

תִּשְׁעָה יַרְחֵי לֵדָה, שְׁמוֹנָה יְמֵי מִילָה,

שִׁבְעָה יְמֵי שַׁבַּתָּא, שִׁשָּׁה סִדְרֵי מִשְׁנָה,

חֲמִשָּׁה חֻמְשֵׁי תוֹרָה, אַרְבַּע אִמָּהוֹת,

שְׁלֹשָׁה אָבוֹת, שְׁנֵי לֻחוֹת הַבְּרִית,

אֶחָד אֱלֹהֵינוּ שֶׁבַּשָּׁמַיִם וּבָאָרֶץ.

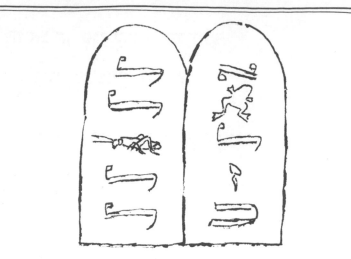

עֲשָׂרָה מִי יוֹדֵעַ? עֲשָׂרָה אֲנִי יוֹדֵעַ:

עֲשָׂרָה דִבְּרַיָּא, תִּשְׁעָה יַרְחֵי לֵדָה,

שְׁמֹנָה יְמֵי מִילָה, שִׁבְעָה יְמֵי שַׁבַּתָּא,

שִׁשָּׁה סִדְרֵי מִשְׁנָה, חֲמִשָּׁה חֻמְשֵׁי תוֹרָה,

אַרְבַּע אִמָּהוֹת, שְׁלֹשָׁה אָבוֹת, שְׁנֵי לֻחוֹת הַבְּרִית,

אֶחָד אֱלֹהֵינוּ שֶׁבַּשָּׁמַיִם וּבָאָרֶץ.

אַחַד עָשָׂר מִי יוֹדֵעַ? אַחַד עָשָׂר אֲנִי יוֹדֵעַ:

אַחַד עָשָׂר כּוֹכְבַיָּא, עֲשָׂרָה דִבְּרַיָּא,

תִּשְׁעָה יַרְחֵי לֵדָה, שְׁמֹנָה יְמֵי מִילָה,

שִׁבְעָה יְמֵי שַׁבַּתָּא, שִׁשָּׁה סִדְרֵי מִשְׁנָה,

חֲמִשָּׁה חֻמְשֵׁי תוֹרָה, אַרְבַּע אִמָּהוֹת,

שְׁלֹשָׁה אָבוֹת, שְׁנֵי לֻחוֹת הַבְּרִית,

אֶחָד אֱלֹהֵינוּ שֶׁבַּשָּׁמַיִם וּבָאָרֶץ.

שְׁנֵים עָשָׂר מִי יוֹדֵעַ? שְׁנֵים עָשָׂר אֲנִי יוֹדֵעַ:

שְׁנֵים עָשָׂר שִׁבְטַיָּא, אַחַד עָשָׂר כּוֹכְבַיָּא,

עֲשָׂרָה דִבְּרַיָּא, תִּשְׁעָה יַרְחֵי לֵדָה,

שְׁמֹנָה יְמֵי מִילָה, שִׁבְעָה יְמֵי שַׁבַּתָּא,

שִׁשָּׁה סִדְרֵי מִשְׁנָה, חֲמִשָּׁה חֻמְשֵׁי תוֹרָה,

אַרְבַּע אִמָּהוֹת, שְׁלֹשָׁה אָבוֹת, שְׁנֵי לֻחוֹת הַבְּרִית,

אֶחָד אֱלֹהֵינוּ שֶׁבַּשָּׁמַיִם וּבָאָרֶץ.

שְׁלֹשָׁה עָשָׂר מִי יוֹדֵעַ? שְׁלֹשָׁה עָשָׂר אֲנִי יוֹדֵעַ:

שְׁלֹשָׁה עָשָׂר מִדַּיָּא, שְׁנֵים עָשָׂר שִׁבְטַיָּא,

אַחַד עָשָׂר כּוֹכְבַיָּא, עֲשָׂרָה דִבְּרַיָּא,

תִּשְׁעָה יַרְחֵי לֵדָה, שְׁמֹנָה יְמֵי מִילָה,

שִׁבְעָה יְמֵי שַׁבַּתָּא, שִׁשָּׁה סִדְרֵי מִשְׁנָה,

חֲמִשָּׁה חֻמְשֵׁי תוֹרָה, אַרְבַּע אִמָּהוֹת,

שְׁלֹשָׁה אָבוֹת, שְׁנֵי לֻחוֹת הַבְּרִית,

אֶחָד אֱלֹהֵינוּ שֶׁבַּשָּׁמַיִם וּבָאָרֶץ.

Who Knows One?

Who knows the meaning of One? I know the meaning of One.
One is God for God is One, the only One in heaven and on earth.

Who knows the meaning of two? I know the meaning of two.
Two tablets of the covenant.
One is God for God is One, the only One in heaven and on earth.

Who knows the meaning of three? I know the meaning of three.
Three patriarchs. Two tablets of the covenant.
One is God for God is One, the only One in heaven and on earth.

Who knows the meaning of four? I know the meaning of four. Four
matriarchs. Three patriarchs. Two tablets of the covenant.
One is God for God is One, the only One in heaven and on earth.

Who knows the meaning of five? I know the meaning of five. Five
books of the Torah. Four matriarchs. Three patriarchs. Two tablets
of the covenant.
One is God for God is One, the only One in heaven and on earth.

Who knows the meaning of six? I know the meaning of six. Six
sections of the Mishnah. Five books of the Torah. Four matriarchs.
Three patriarchs. Two tablets of the covenant.
One is God for God is One, the only One in heaven and on earth.

Who knows the meaning of seven? I know the meaning of seven.
Seven days of the week. Six sections of the Mishnah. Five books
of the Torah. Four matriarchs. Three patriarchs. Two tablets of the
covenant.
One is God for God is One, the only One in heaven and on earth.

Who knows the meaning of eight? I know the meaning of eight.
Eight days till circumcision. Seven days of the week. Six sections
of the Mishnah. Five books of the Torah. Four matriarchs. Three
patriarchs. Two tablets of the covenant.
One is God for God is One, the only One in heaven and on earth.

Who knows the meaning of nine? I know the meaning of nine. Nine months of pregnancy. Eight days till circumcision. Seven days of the week. Six sections of the Mishnah. Five books of the Torah. Four matriarchs. Three patriarchs. Two tablets of the covenant.

One is God for God is One, the only One in heaven and on earth.

Who knows the meaning of ten? I know the meaning of ten. Ten commandments. Nine months of pregnancy. Eight days till circumcision. Seven days of the week. Six sections of the Mishnah. Five books of the Torah. Four matriarchs. Three patriarchs. Two tablets of the covenant.

One is God for God is One, the only One in heaven and on earth.

Who knows the meaning of eleven? I know the meaning of eleven. Eleven stars in Joseph's dream. Ten commandments. Nine months of pregnancy. Eight days till circumcision. Seven days of the week. Six sections of the Mishnah. Five books of the Torah. Four matriarchs. Three patriarchs. Two tablets of the covenant.

One is God for God is One, the only One in heaven and on earth.

Who knows the meaning of twelve? I know the meaning of twelve. Twelve tribes. Eleven stars in Joseph's dream. Ten commandments. Nine months of pregnancy. Eight days till circumcision. Seven days of the week. Six sections of the Mishnah. Five books of the Torah. Four matriarchs. Three patriarchs. Two tablets of the covenant.

One is God for God is One, the only One in heaven and on earth.

Who knows the meaning of thirteen? I know the meaning of thirteen. Thirteen attributes of God. Twelve tribes. Eleven stars in Joseph's dream. Ten commandments. Nine months of pregnancy. Eight days till circumcision. Seven days of the week. Six sections of the Mishnah. Five books of the Torah. Four matriarchs. Three patriarchs. Two tablets of the covenant.

One is God for God is One, the only One in heaven and on earth.

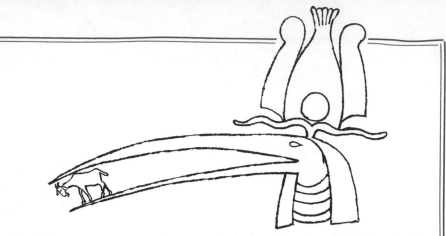

And here we are, ready to conclude with *Chad Gadya*. This beautiful, innocent song tells the story of a father who buys a little goat for his son. But everything goes wrong: God's creatures wound and devour one another, the elements try to destroy one another . . .

What a puzzling way to end a joyous meal. Is it intended to illustrate the workings of divine justice? Or to arouse compassion for the little goat? The song evokes the destiny of the Jewish people; that is clear. But who symbolizes the Jewish people? The goat? Surely not, for he disappears. Rather, the Jewish people is symbolized by the child who receives the goat. The child, though saddened by the goat's disappearance, remains till the end. But when is that? The end is when death is defeated. The end is the death of death.

And where is love in all this? And where is joy? And redemption? They are there. They are in the relationship between the child and the goat, between the goat and the song, and between the father and all of them, all of us.

The real meaning of the song may be that, in Jewish history, all creatures, all beings, all events are connected. The goat and the cat, the fire and the water, the slaughterer and the redeemer are all part of the story.

Sometimes stories are sad. Still, it is important to tell them and retell them, to live them again and again, this year and next, when we shall meet again around this Seder table.

חַד גַּדְיָא

חַד גַּדְיָא, חַד גַּדְיָא,

דְּזַבַּן אַבָּא בִּתְרֵי זוּזֵי.

חַד גַּדְיָא, חַד גַּדְיָא.

וְאָתָא שׁוּנְרָא וְאָכַל לְגַדְיָא,

דְּזַבַּן אַבָּא בִּתְרֵי זוּזֵי.

חַד גַּדְיָא, חַד גַּדְיָא.

וְאָתָא כַלְבָּא וְנָשַׁךְ לְשׁוּנְרָא,

דְּאָכַל לְגַדְיָא, דְּזַבַּן אַבָּא בִּתְרֵי זוּזֵי.

חַד גַּדְיָא, חַד גַּדְיָא.

וְאָתָא חוּטְרָא וְהִכָּה לְכַלְבָּא,

דְּנָשַׁךְ לְשׁוּנְרָא, דְּאָכַל לְגַדְיָא,

דְּזַבַּן אַבָּא בִּתְרֵי זוּזֵי.

חַד גַּדְיָא, חַד גַּדְיָא.

וְאָתָא נוּרָא וְשָׂרַף לְחוּטְרָא,

דְּהִכָּה לְכַלְבָּא, דְּנָשַׁךְ לְשׁוּנְרָא,

דְּאָכַל לְגַדְיָא, דְּזַבֵּן אַבָּא בִּתְרֵי זוּזֵי.

חַד גַּדְיָא, חַד גַּדְיָא.

וְאָתָא מַיָּא וְכָבָה לְנוּרָא,

דְּשָׂרַף לְחוּטְרָא, דְּהִכָּה לְכַלְבָּא,

דְּנָשַׁךְ לְשׁוּנְרָא, דְּאָכַל לְגַדְיָא,

דְּזַבֵּן אַבָּא בִּתְרֵי זוּזֵי.

חַד גַּדְיָא, חַד גַּדְיָא.

וְאָתָא תוֹרָא וְשָׁתָה לְמַיָּא,

דְּכָבָה לְנוּרָא, דְּשָׂרַף לְחוּטְרָא,

דְּהִכָּה לְכַלְבָּא, דְּנָשַׁךְ לְשׁוּנְרָא,

דְּאָכַל לְגַדְיָא, דְּזַבֵּן אַבָּא בִּתְרֵי זוּזֵי.

חַד גַּדְיָא, חַד גַּדְיָא.

וְאָתָא הַשׁוֹחֵט וְשָׁחַט לְתוֹרָא,

דְּשָׁתָא לְמַיָּא, דְּכָבָה לְנוּרָא,

דְּשָׂרַף לְחוּטְרָא, דְּהִכָּה לְכַלְבָּא,

דְּנָשַׁךְ לְשׁוּנְרָא, דְּאָכַל לְגַדְיָא,

דְּזַבַן אַבָּא בִּתְרֵי זוּזֵי.

חַד גַּדְיָא, חַד גַּדְיָא.

וְאָתָא מַלְאַךְ הַמָּוֶת, וְשָׁחַט לְשׁוֹחֵט,

דְּשָׁחַט לְתוֹרָא, דְּשָׁתָה לְמַיָּא,

דְּכָבָה לְנוּרָא, דְּשָׂרַף לְחוּטְרָא,

דְּהִכָּה לְכַלְבָּא, דְּנָשַׁךְ לְשׁוּנְרָא,

דְּאָכַל לְגַדְיָא, דְּזַבַן אַבָּא בִּתְרֵי זוּזֵי.

חַד גַּדְיָא, חַד גַּדְיָא.

וְאָתָא הַקָּדוֹשׁ בָּרוּךְ הוּא, וְשָׁחַט לְמַלְאַךְ הַמָּוֶת,

דְּשָׁחַט לְשׁוֹחֵט, דְּשָׁחַט לְתוֹרָא,

דְּשָׁתָה לְמַיָּא, דְּכָבָה לְנוּרָא,

דְּשָׂרַף לְחוּטְרָא, דְּהִכָּה לְכַלְבָּא,

דְּנָשַׁךְ לְשׁוּנְרָא, דְּאָכַל לְגַדְיָא,

דְּזַבַן אַבָּא בִּתְרֵי זוּזֵי.

חַד גַּדְיָא, חַד גַּדְיָא.

One Little Goat

There was one little goat. One very little goat that my father bought
   for two zuzim.
One little goat. One very little goat.

Then came a cat and ate the goat that my father bought for two
   zuzim.
One little goat. One very little goat.

Then came a dog and bit the cat that ate the goat that my father
   bought for two zuzim.
One little goat. One very little goat.

Then came a stick and beat the dog that bit the cat that ate the
   goat that my father bought for two zuzim.
One little goat. One very little goat.

Then came a fire and burned the stick that beat the dog that bit the
   cat that ate the goat that my father bought for two zuzim.
One little goat. One very little goat.

Then came the water and quenched the fire that burned the stick
   that beat the dog that bit the cat that ate the goat that my father
   bought for two zuzim.
One little goat. One very little goat.

Then came the ox and drank the water that quenched the fire that
   burned the stick that beat the dog that bit the cat that ate the
   goat that my father bought for two zuzim.
One little goat. One very little goat.

Then came the slaughterer and slaughtered the ox that drank the water that quenched the fire that burned the stick that beat the dog that bit the cat that ate the goat that my father bought for two zuzim.

One little goat. One very little goat.

Then came the angel of death and killed the slaughterer who slaughtered the ox that drank the water that quenched the fire that burned the stick that beat the dog that bit the cat that ate the goat that my father bought for two zuzim.

One little goat. One very little goat.

Then came God, blessed be His name, and He slew the angel of death who killed the slaughterer who slaughtered the ox that drank the water that quenched the fire that burned the stick that beat the dog that bit the cat that ate the goat that my father bought for two zuzim.

One little goat. One very little goat.